GRADE 3

WONDERFUL WORD STUDY ACTIVITIES

100 Independent Practice Pages That Expand Vocabulary Across Content Areas

AMANDA NEHRING

SCHOLASTIC

SVP & Publisher: Tara Welty
Executive Editorial Director: Sarah Longhi
Editors: Michelle Sturm, Lynne M. Wilson
Cover design: Cynthia Ng
Interior design: Grafica, Inc.
Illustrations: Doug Jones, Rob McClurkan
Stock photos © Shutterstock.com

ISBN: 978-1-5461-5257-6
Scholastic Inc., 557 Broadway, New York, NY 10012

Printed in the U.S.A.
First printing, January 2026.

1 2 3 4 5 6 7 8 9 10 40 35 34 33 32 31 30 29 28 27 26

Table of Contents

Welcome to Wonderful Word Study Activities: Grade 3!

The 100 reproducible word games and activities in this book provide you and your students with quick and fun ways to build robust content-area vocabulary. The activities come in two-page packets that each focus on a specific skill or topic in English language arts, science, or social studies. You can use the two pages together or separately as best meets your needs and goals. These engaging vocabulary-building activities make learning motivating and invite students to discover that words can be both powerful and fun to explore!

Research tells us that students' reading comprehension and knowledge-building improve as their understanding of content-area vocabulary increases.[1] The topics and words for *Wonderful Word Study Activities* align with national and state-level third-grade standards and core curricula. You'll find a range of academic and content-area vocabulary that students are likely to encounter in grade-level texts.

The activities in these packets include traditional puzzle types, such as crossword puzzles and word searches, context- and definition-based activities, and word games that spark creative thinking and problem-solving. These word puzzles and games aren't just engaging and fun—they are also powerful tools for building vocabulary and language.

Here's a closer look at the activity types and their benefits:

- **Word scramble puzzles**, including word wheels, help students develop word-recognition skills, spelling, and creative thinking. Many activities culminate with an unscramble challenge that reveals the answer to a riddle or question.
- **Word searches** are a proven method for reinforcing students' pattern-recognition skills, boosting spelling ability, and increasing retention of content-area terms.[2]

---

[1] Trane, F. E., Rivas, M. J., & Jones, M. R. (2022). *The Science of Reading: What research says about setting young readers up for success.* WestEd.

[2] Fitria, T. N. "The Effectiveness of Word Search Puzzles Game in Improving Students' Vocabulary." *Pioneer: Journal of Language and Literature*, vol. 15, no. 1, 30 June 2023, pp. 50-67.

- **Using words in context** is a real-world way of exploring vocabulary. As students read sentences and fill in the blanks with appropriate words, they will build comprehension skills and background knowledge.
- **Word sorts** challenge students to exercise their reasoning skills and think about how words and ideas relate to one another. In these activities, students group words into categories, identify words that don't belong in a set, or use characteristics of words to solve a maze. Then students must explain their answers, encouraging critical thinking and fostering vocabulary retention.
- **A synonym and antonym spinner** gives students practice with both new and familiar vocabulary words as they think about how words relate to each other. This activity also provides opportunities for discussions about word choice and nuances of meaning.
- **Crossword puzzles** boost vocabulary and motivation for learning as students use definitions and clues to fit words into the puzzle.[3] Students must consider multiple meanings, word length, and spelling to properly interlock the words.
- **Cryptograms** target logic skills and tap into students' understanding of how letters are arranged within words. These code-breaking activities reinforce language skills, spelling, and pattern recognition.
- **Constructing words with Greek and Latin roots** raises students' morphological awareness. Enhancing students' ability to identify meaningful parts of words, such as roots, prefixes, and suffixes, can effectively double or triple their vocabularies. And as students tackle increasingly complex content-area words, familiarity with these roots will serve as an important foundation for reading comprehension.
- **Word builder** challenges, in which students create as many words as possible from the letters in a longer word or phrase, employ higher-order thinking skills. Students not only build spelling skills and word recall but also explore the ideas behind the words by identifying which ones relate to the original phrase.

You can use these activities as morning starters, fast-finisher activities, homework, or meaningful independent practice while you work with small groups. The packets are particularly helpful as part of a unit wrap-up since students will have the background knowledge to more deeply play with, think about, and make connections with the words and ideas in each activity.

---

[3] Orawiwatnakul, W. (2013). "Crossword puzzles as a learning tool for vocabulary development." *Electronic Journal of Research in Educational Psychology*, vol. 11, no. 2, 2013, pp. 413-428.

While students can complete these packets independently, consider engaging them in conversations about their answers. Invite them to share their thinking with you (and with one another) to further strengthen their understanding and help them make even more connections among the words and ideas. Making these connections is an important part of increasing students' vocabulary, knowledge, and reading skills. Where more than one correct answer is possible, accept any reasonable answer. Your interest in and encouragement of your students' ideas and solutions will build their verbal reasoning skills and confidence both in and out of the classroom.

As students complete these pages, they can experience the joy of more deeply understanding word meanings while practicing key skills. These skills, such as following directions and problem-solving, help boost testing success and broader academic growth. More important, the satisfaction and confidence that your students gain as they solve tricky word challenges will boost their resilience, perseverance, and motivation to become lifelong learners.

Enjoy!

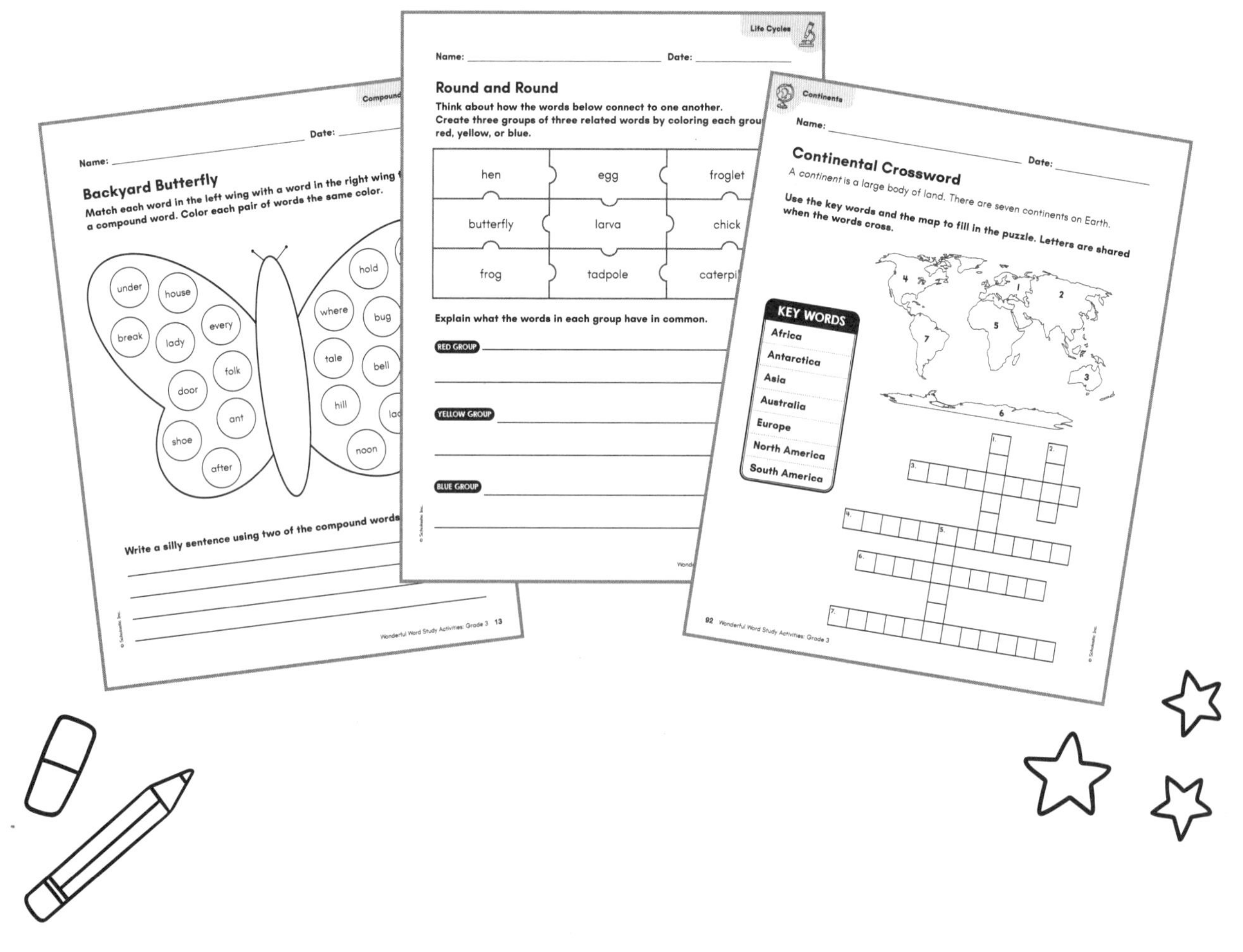

Meeting Core Language Arts Standards

The activities in this book meet the following English language arts standards for grade 3.

CONVENTIONS OF STANDARD ENGLISH	
L.3.1.B	Form and use regular and irregular plural nouns.
L.3.2.D	Form and use possessives.
L.3.2.E	Use conventional spelling for high-frequency and other studied words and for adding suffixes to base words (e.g., *sitting, smiled, cries, happiness*).
VOCABULARY ACQUISITION AND USE	
L.3.4	Determine or clarify the meaning of unknown and multiple-meaning words and phrases based on grade 3 reading and content, choosing flexibly from a range of strategies.
L.3.4.A	Use sentence-level context as a clue to the meaning of a word or phrase.
L.3.4.C	Use a known root word as a clue to the meaning of an unknown word with the same root (e.g., *company, companion*).
L.3.5	Demonstrate understanding of figurative language, word relationships, and nuances in word meanings.
L.3.5.A	Distinguish the literal and nonliteral meanings of words and phrases in context (e.g., *take steps*).
L.3.6	Acquire and use accurately grade-appropriate conversational, general academic, and domain-specific words and phrases, including those that signal spatial and temporal relationships (e.g., *After dinner that night we went looking for them*).
PHONICS AND WORD RECOGNITION	
RF.3.3	Know and apply grade-level phonics and word analysis skills in decoding words.
RF.3.3.B	Decode words with common Latin suffixes.
RF.3.3.C	Decode multisyllable words.
RF.3.3.D	Read grade-appropriate irregularly spelled words.
CRAFT AND STRUCTURE	
RI.3.4	Determine the meaning of general academic and domain-specific words and phrases in a text relevant to a grade 3 topic or subject area.

Name: ________________________ Date: ______________

In Plain Sight

Some words show up a lot in reading and writing. Practicing them helps us recognize them more quickly. You can learn them by looking closely at their letters and sounds and using them in sentences.

KEY WORDS

about	**bring**	**laugh**	**myself**
right	**said**	**very**	**would**

Put a star next to the key words you recognized right away. Sound out each of the other words. Then use the key words to complete the sentences below.

1. I read a story ___ ___ ___ ___ (___) a talking dog.
2. José's silly joke made us ___ (___) ___ ___ ___ out loud.
3. I (___) ___ ___ ___ ___ love to go to the park on Saturday.
4. Please ___ (___) ___ ___ ___ your favorite book to read.
5. I learned to skateboard all by ___ ___ ___ (___) ___ ___.
6. Alan got all the ___ (___) ___ ___ ___ answers on the test.
7. The soup is ___ (___) ___ ___ hot, so be careful.
8. Aunt Judy ___ ___ ___ (___) we will have pizza for dinner.

Why are these words important to know?
Unscramble the circled letters to find out.

They help us r___ ___ ___ and ___ ___ ___ ___ ___ well.

Name: ______________________ Date: ______________

Spot the Words!

Find the key words in the puzzle. Words can go → or ↓.

WORD BANK

about	bring	laugh	myself
right	said	very	would

h	j	e	n	b	s	a	i	d	k
v	e	r	y	t	s	e	f	x	i
q	i	a	r	n	f	e	q	s	d
z	e	a	k	r	d	k	s	t	w
q	i	b	r	i	n	g	t	i	u
e	z	o	u	g	h	k	y	m	e
q	k	u	l	h	x	w	p	t	p
x	a	t	i	t	w	o	u	l	d
t	y	l	a	y	b	l	q	a	s
s	a	i	k	n	r	m	e	u	y
p	m	y	s	e	l	f	z	g	v
m	j	g	b	h	r	i	d	h	x

Name: ______________________ **Date:** ______________

A Famous Voyage

High-frequency words are words that show up a lot in movies, books, and when people talk to each other. Learning these words makes it easier to understand stories, such as the one below about a *voyage*, or long journey.

KEY WORDS

around	**below**	**between**	**could**
few	**how**	**many**	**where**

Put a star next to the key words you recognized right away. Sound out each of the other words. Then use the key words to complete the sentences below. You will use each word only once.

1. Jeanne Baret was the first woman to sail ______________ the world.

2. ______________ others had tried, but she actually did it!

3. Very ______________ people in the 1700s knew her name.

4. I wonder ______________ long it took her to complete the voyage.

5. ______________ did her boat leave from?

6. Did she sail ______________ icebergs or continents?

7. Was there a place to rest ______________ the deck?

8. I ______________ check out a book from the library to find out!

Name: ______________________ Date: ______________

Sort It Out

Think about how the words below connect to one another. Create three groups of three related words by coloring each group red, yellow, or blue.

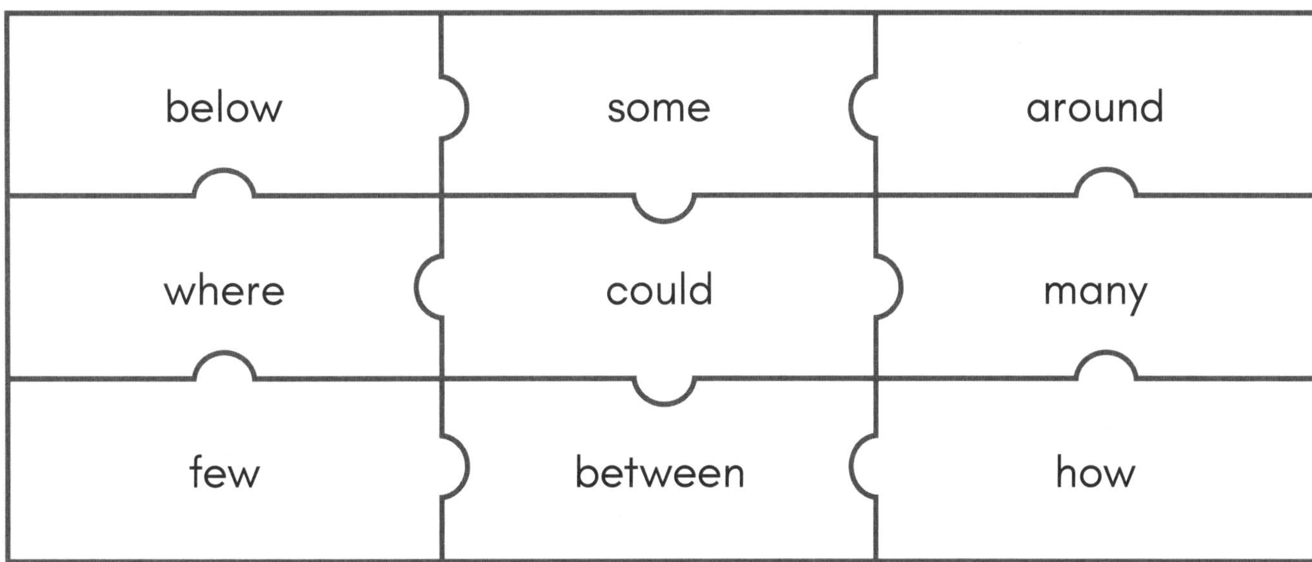

below	some	around
where	could	many
few	between	how

Explain what the words in each group have in common.

RED GROUP ______________________________

____

YELLOW GROUP ______________________________

____

BLUE GROUP ______________________________

____

Name: ______________________ Date: ______________

Compound Matchup

A *compound word* is formed when two smaller words are put together to create a new word.

Match each compound word below with its meaning.

1. underground	**A.** a button near a door that makes a sound
2. ladybug	**B.** a long string used to tie a shoe
3. shoelace	**C.** in all places
4. household	**D.** below the dirt
5. everywhere	**E.** between noon and night
6. anthill	**F.** a small red-and-black insect
7. doorbell	**G.** a small dirt pile where tiny insects live
8. toothbrush	**H.** light in the daytime sky
9. sunshine	**I.** a small tool used to clean teeth
10. afternoon	**J.** people who live together in a home

Name: ______________________________ Date: ________________

Backyard Butterfly

Match each word in the left wing with a word in the right wing to make a compound word. Color each pair of words the same color.

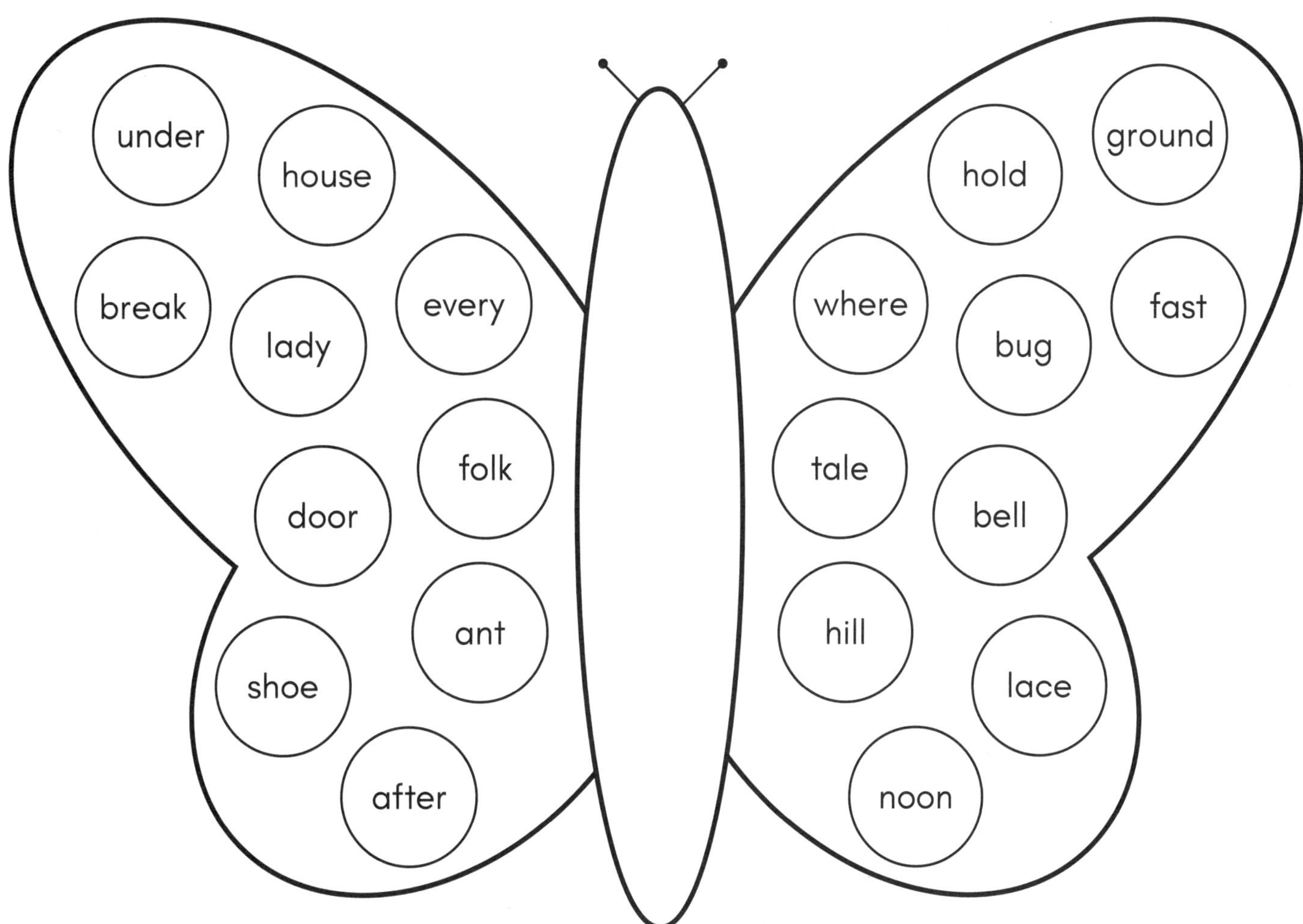

Write a silly sentence using two of the compound words.

____

____

____

____

Name: ______________________ **Date:** ______________

Happy Homophones

Homophones are words that sound exactly alike but have different spellings and meanings. Knowing the right meaning for each spelling is important. It helps you choose the right word when you are writing.

Match each of the words on the left to its homophone.

1. flower	**A.** tide
2. write	**B.** mane
3. plain	**C.** site
4. main	**D.** night
5. pair	**E.** plane
6. sight	**F.** pear
7. knight	**G.** blew
8. blue	**H.** flour
9. tied	**I.** right

Write a silly sentence using one pair of homophones.

____

Name: ______________________ **Date:** ______________

The Right Word to Write

Circle the correct word to complete each sentence.

1. Justine **cent sent scent** a letter to her grandfather last Friday.
2. I sure hope the tooth **fairy ferry** can find my house tonight!
3. We must hammer the nail carefully into the **bored board**.
4. Tío Rodrigo called a **toe tow** truck when his car ran out of gas.
5. Grandpa left the bread **dough doe** on the counter to rise.
6. Have you **seen scene** my other shoe? I can't find it!

Draw a silly picture of a pair of homophones.

Name: ______________________________ **Date:** ________________

Plenty of Plurals

A *plural* word shows that there is more than one of something. Some plural words are formed by changing the spelling of the singular word. Here are three rules for making plural words:

1. For most words, just add *s*.
2. If the word ends in *ch*, *sh*, *s*, *x*, or *z*, add *es* instead.
3. If the word's last letter is *y*, change the *y* to an *i* and add *es*.

KEY WORDS

bird	bunny	cat	fox	giraffe
guppy	lizard	ostrich	pony	puppy

Write the plural form of each key word in the correct column.

ADD *S*	ADD *ES*	CHANGE *Y* TO *I* AND ADD *ES*

Name: ______________________ Date: ______________

Plurals on Parade

Complete the story below. Use the picture clues to write the plural form of each key word on the correct line.

KEY WORDS

bird	box	bunny
bus	cat	dish
hat	iguana	puppy

This Saturday, we will have our first pet parade! It will star cute

________________ on leashes. There will also be adorable

______________ in ______________ . My friend Miguel will

bring his four ________________ . They will ride on the toy

______________ that he decorated. The ________________ and

________________ will sit on top of treat ______________ or

special ______________ . It's going to be a great day!

Name: ______________________ **Date:** ______________

Contraction Maze

A contraction uses an apostrophe to combine two words into one. The apostrophe replaces one or more letters from the original words. For example, she + is = she's.

The apostrophe in a possessive noun shows who something belongs to, as in "Olivia's jacket."

Help the pirates get to the treasure chest. Draw a line by following the contractions. Don't go through the possessive nouns. They're traps!

it's	teacher's	cat's	Sara's
we're	I'm	book's	school's
Florida's	they've	you're	he'll
dog's	unicorn's	game's	she'll
tree's	roof's	scooter's	can't

Name: ______________________ Date: ______________

Does This Belong to Someone?

An apostrophe can show that two words have been put together to make a contraction. It can also make a noun possessive, showing you that something belongs to the noun.

KEY WORDS

elephants'	**he's**	**I'm**
Leilani's	**library's**	**New York's**
she'd	**you're**	**zebra's**

Write the key word that best completes each sentence on the lines below. Circle C if the word is a contraction and P if it is a possessive noun.

1. I like to run. ____________ really fast! **C / P**
2. ____________ dog loves to walk with her. **C / P**
3. ____________ invited, and I hope you can come. **C / P**
4. I like my teacher, Mr. Barrett, because ____________ funny. **C / P**
5. The ____________ trunks are long and wrinkled. **C / P**
6. The Statue of Liberty is one of ____________ famous sites. **C / P**
7. My little sister said ____________ like to ride her bike. **C / P**
8. We love the ____________ summer reading program. **C / P**

Write a sentence using the unused key word.

____

____

Name: ______________________ Date: ______________

Working Words

Words have different jobs in a sentence. Some words name things, some show action, and others describe things or make connections.

KEY WORDS

adjective	**adverb**	**article**	**conjunction**
noun	**preposition**	**pronoun**	**verb**

Read the definitions. Then unscramble the letters to spell each word.

1. ctjiveade ______________ describes a noun

2. vdrabe ______________ describes a verb, adjective, or another adverb

3. tleirca ______________ a little word that comes before a noun

4. ncutonjocin ______________ connects words or ideas

5. unno ______________ a word that names a person, place, thing, or idea

6. pienotrpiso ______________ a word that tells where or when something is

7. nrouonp ______________ a word that takes the place of a noun

8. brve ______________ a word that tells an action or a state of being

Name: ______________________ Date: ______________

Color Mr. Turtle

Use the key to color each word on Mr. Turtle's shell. You'll use a different color for each part of speech.

IF THE WORD IS A/AN...	COLOR IT...
adjective	blue
conjunction	brown
noun	green
preposition	purple
pronoun	orange
verb	red

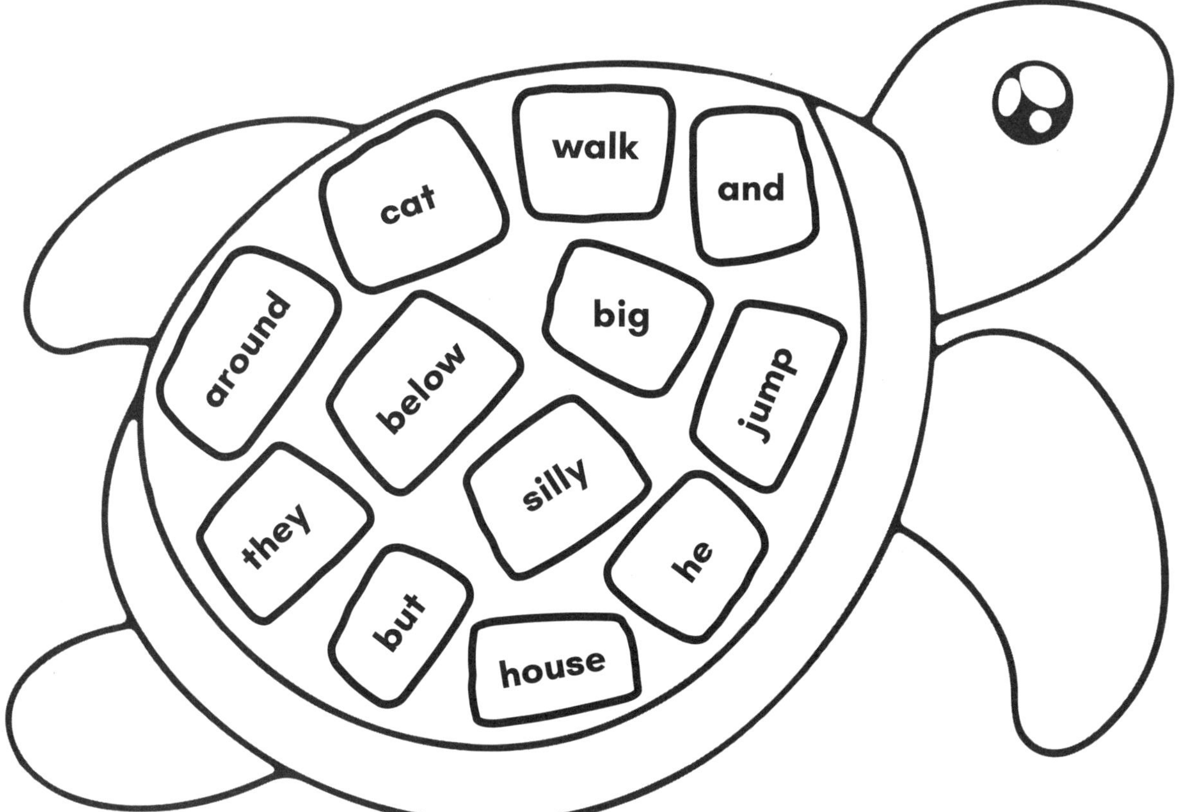

Name: ______________________ **Date:** ______________

Sensational Similes

A *simile* uses *like* or *as* to make a comparison between two different things.

KEY WORDS

cloud	giraffe	ice
owl	rocket	turtle

Use the key words to complete the sentences.
You will use each word only once.

1. Vic solved the puzzle as wisely as an ______________.

2. The marble floor was cold like ______________.

3. My baby sister crawled as slowly as a ______________.

4. Jamal zoomed past us like a ______________ on the playground.

5. The basketball player was as tall as a ______________.

6. His blanket was soft like a ______________.

Write your own sentence using a simile.

____

____

Name: ______________________ **Date:** ______________

Spin a Simile

For each of the sets of nouns below, spin the spinner. Use the word it lands on to write a simile that compares the two nouns. The first one has been done for you.

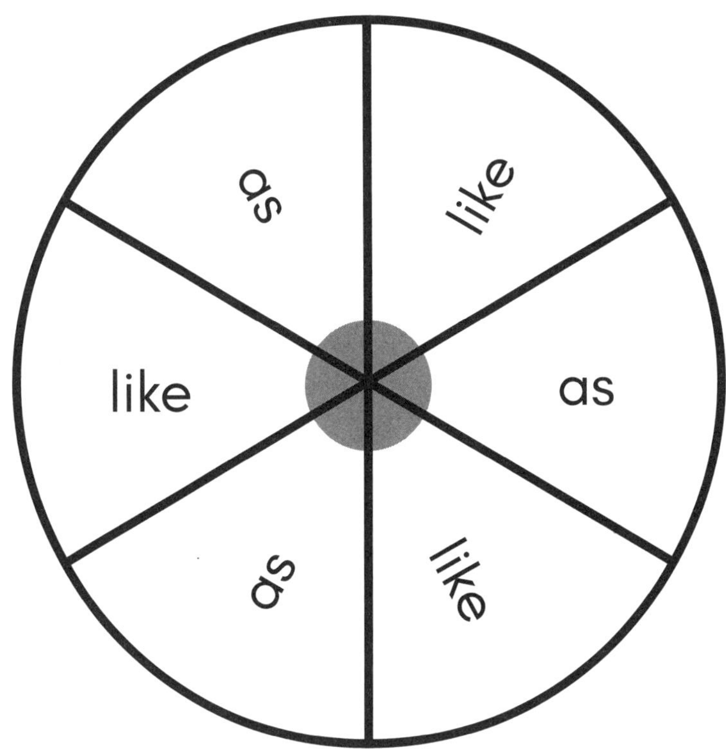

Place a pencil and a paper clip at the center of the spinner, as shown. Flick the paper clip to spin the spinner.

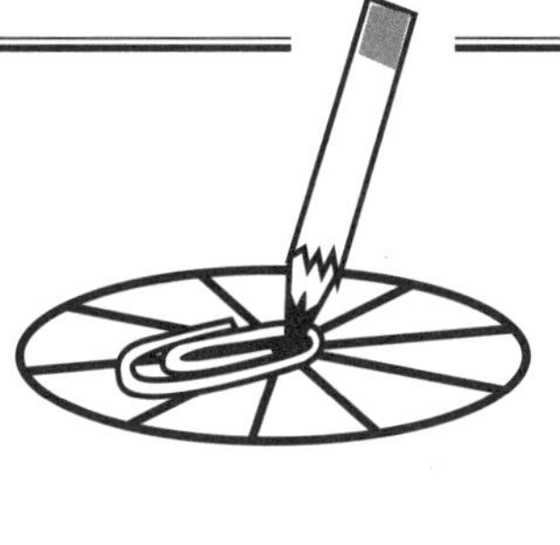

1. fur, velvet The cat's fur was as smooth as velvet.
2. rock, ball ______________________
3. flashlight, sun ______________________
4. eyes, sky ______________________
5. child, mouse ______________________
6. blanket, grass ______________________

Name: ____________________ Date: ____________

What Does It Mean?

Idioms are phrases people use to make their writing more interesting. The words say one thing but mean something else.

Match each idiom with its meaning.

1. let the cat out of the bag	**A.** be patient
2. two peas in a pod	**B.** working really hard
3. the eleventh hour	**C.** something very expensive
4. get cold feet	**D.** tell a secret by accident
5. busy as a bee	**E.** two people who are very similar
6. hold your horses	**F.** help someone
7. on cloud nine	**G.** feel scared or nervous about something
8. lend a hand	**H.** the last minute
9. cost an arm and a leg	**I.** feeling very happy

Choose one of the idioms above. On a separate piece of paper, make two drawings. First, draw what the words say. Then, draw what the idiom means.

Name: ______________________ Date: ______________

More Than Meets the Words

Think about how the idioms below connect to one another. Create three groups of three related idioms by coloring each group red, yellow, or blue.

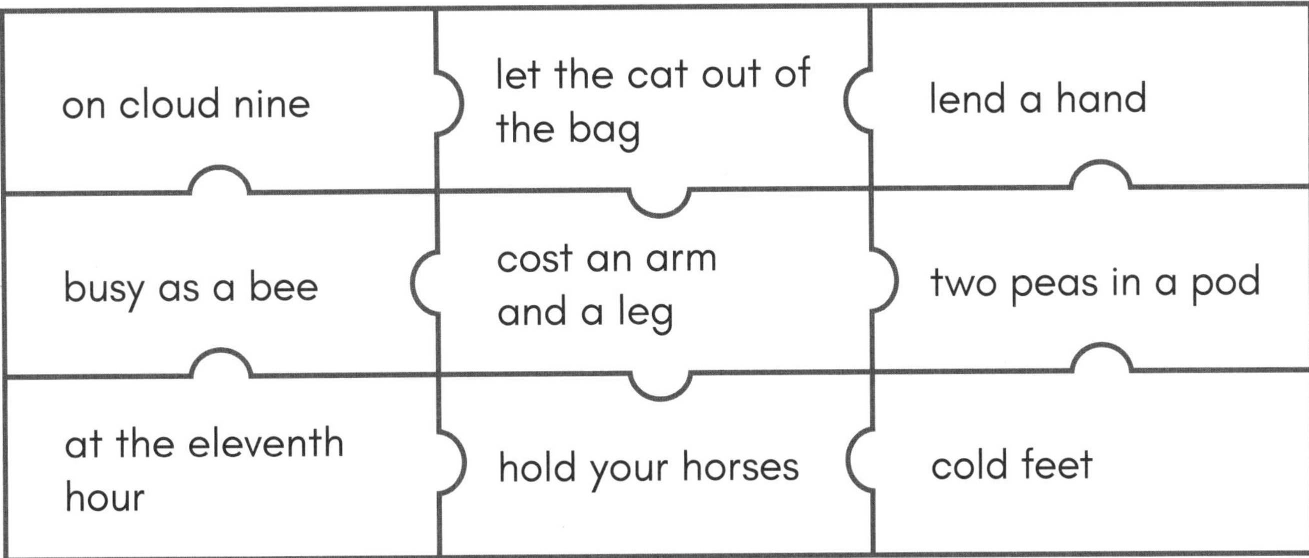

Explain what the idioms in each group have in common.

RED GROUP ______________________________

____

YELLOW GROUP ______________________________

____

BLUE GROUP ______________________________

____

Name: ______________________ **Date:** ______________

Undercover Words

There are many *genres*, or kinds, of stories. Some are funny or make-believe. Others are full of facts. Knowing the genre can help you understand what you're reading.

Use the key words to fill in the puzzle. Letters are shared when the words cross.

KEY WORDS

- fable
- fiction
- folktale
- graphic novel
- myth
- nonfiction
- play
- poetry

ACROSS

1. Writing that is true and gives facts
4. A story with pictures and speech bubbles
6. A tale about gods or how things came to be
7. A story performed on stage by actors
8. A short tale in which animals teach a lesson

DOWN

2. A made-up story
3. An old story passed down over time
5. Words written with rhythm and sometimes rhyme

Name: ______________________ **Date:** ______________

What's My Genre?

Use the Code Breaker Key to solve the riddles and reveal four literary genres.

CODE BREAKER KEY

A	B	C	D	E	F	G	H	I	J	K	L	M
N	**O**	**P**	**Q**	**R**	**S**	**T**	**U**	**V**	**W**	**X**	**Y**	**Z**

1. Talking cars in high-speed races,
Made-up people, made-up places.

2. From dino facts to the sun's bright light,
I tell what's real, what's true, what's right.

3. I'm written to perform and share.
Actors read me with drama and flair.

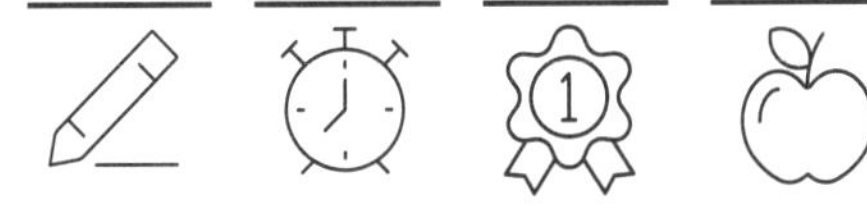

4. I can be short and sweet.
Rhythm and rhyme help me feel complete.

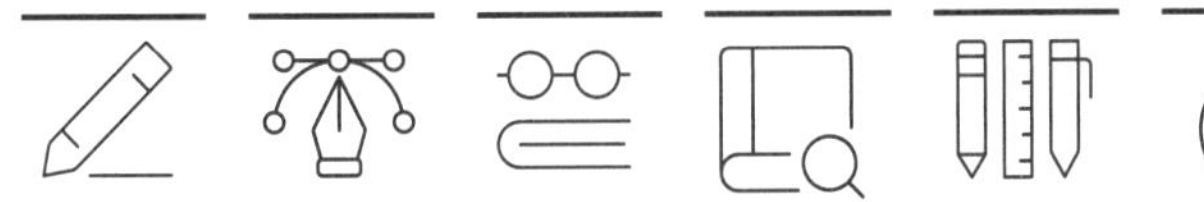

Name: ______________________________ **Date:** ______________

Find the Facts

Nonfiction texts provide facts about a topic. You can use them to do research and learn about new things.

KEY WORDS

authors	**conclusion**	**evidence**
fact	**opinion**	**primary**
questions	**research**	**secondary**

Use the key words to complete the sentences below. You will use each word only once.

1. A ___ ___ (___) ___ is something that can be proven true.
2. A diary or photo is a ___ ___ ___ ___ (___) ___ ___ source.
3. Writers of books and articles are called ___ ___ ___ ___ ___ ___ (___).
4. A textbook is a ___ (___) ___ ___ ___ ___ ___ ___ ___ source.
5. Researchers use facts and evidence to come to a (___) ___ ___ ___ (___) ___ ___ ___ ___ ___.
6. An ___ ___ ___ ___ ___ (___) ___ is a person's thoughts or feelings about something.
7. When you study a topic to learn more, you are doing ___ ___ (___) ___ ___ ___ ___ ___.
8. You can find answers to many ___ ___ (___) ___ ___ ___ ___ ___ ___ in nonfiction texts.
9. You gather ___ ___ ___ (___) ___ ___ ___ ___ when you do research.

What did the researcher say when she solved the mystery? Write the circled letters in order to find out.

___ ___ ___ ___   ___ ___ ___ ___ ___ ___!

Name: ______________________________ Date: ______________

Research Roundup

Find the key words about research in the puzzle. Words can go → or ↓.

WORD BANK

author	conclusion	evidence	fact
opinion	primary	research	secondary

d	r	t	o	i	f	a	c	t	o
c	p	r	i	m	a	r	y	h	c
r	t	x	c	b	o	r	a	q	o
e	v	i	d	e	n	c	e	n	n
s	e	c	o	n	d	a	r	y	c
e	f	r	t	o	x	l	z	e	l
a	u	t	h	o	r	f	a	r	u
r	n	z	o	r	m	d	t	i	s
c	o	e	n	m	f	r	r	y	i
h	e	c	l	a	i	t	s	a	o
d	z	t	d	e	i	u	q	p	n
s	r	w	o	p	i	n	i	o	n

Name: ______________________ Date: ______________

What's the Author Up To?

Authors write for different reasons. Sometimes they want to tell a funny story, share facts, or try to change your mind. That's called an *author's purpose*.

For each book title, write *inform*, *entertain*, or *persuade* to show the author's purpose. Then draw a book cover that matches the title.

BOOK TITLE	AUTHOR'S PURPOSE	BOOK COVER
Why You Should Adopt 10 Puppies		
How to Make a Paper Airplane		
Harold, the Talking Banana		

Name: ______________________ Date: ______________

What Am I Writing and Why?

One letter is missing from each wheel below. Figure out where each word starts. Then add one key letter to complete it.

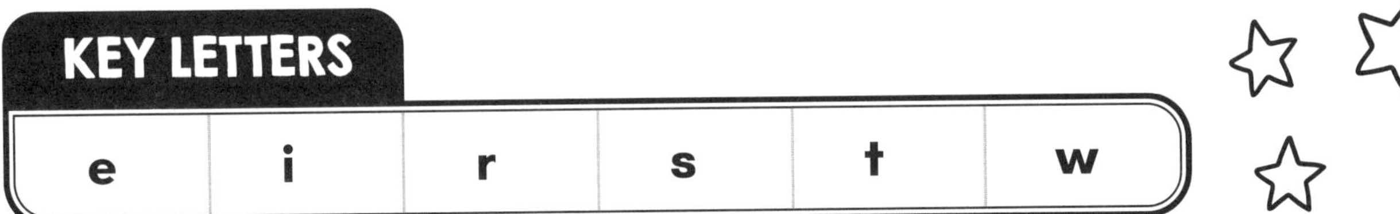

1. n e s p a p e r
2. t o y s
3. c p e r e
4. i c l e s a r
5. s j o k
6. r l e t t e

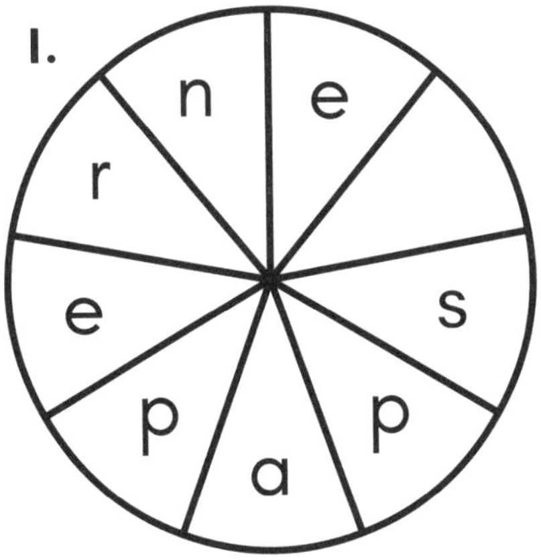

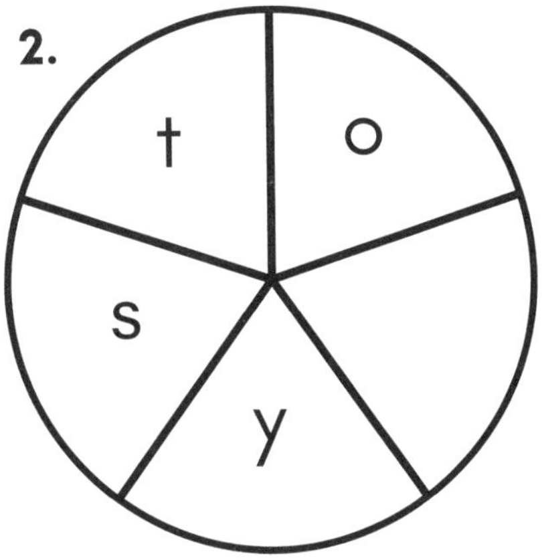

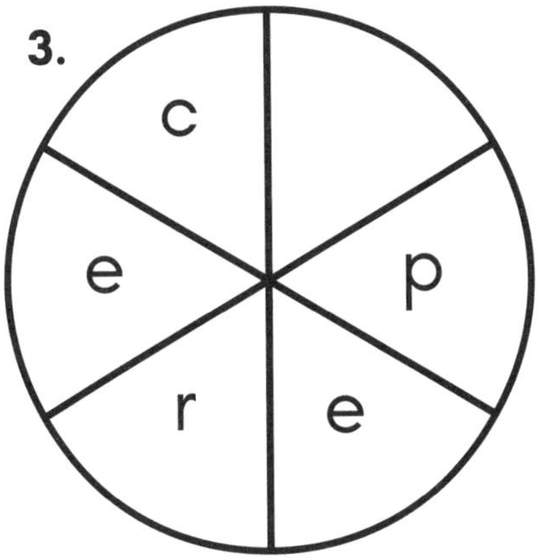

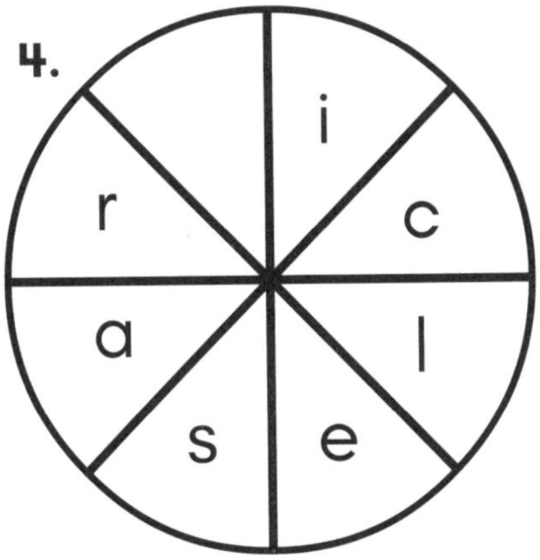

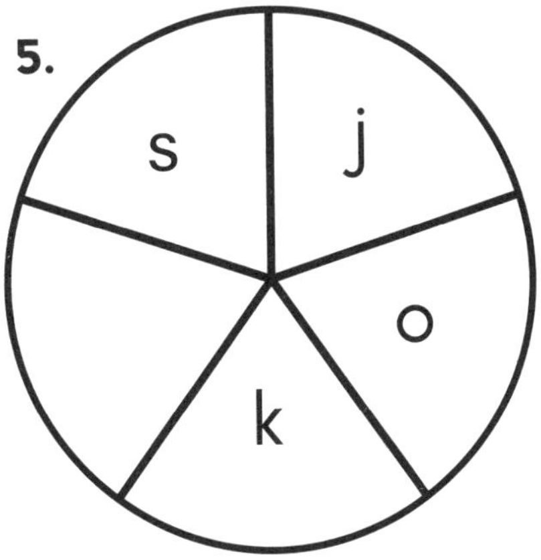

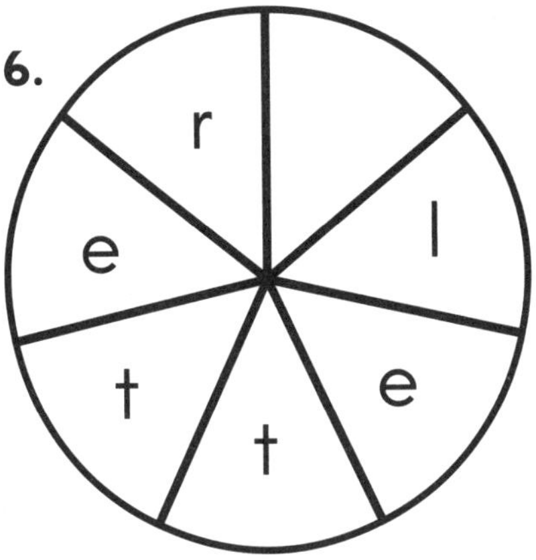

Write the missing letters in order to complete this sentence about author's purpose.

An author ___ ___ ___ ___ ___ ___ to persuade,

entertain, or inform.

Name: ______________________ **Date:** ______________

Word Detective

Understanding new words can be tricky. The words and sentences around the word can help you figure out its meaning. These clues are called *context clues.*

Write each bold word from the paragraph next to its definition below.

Olivia wanted to get to know the new boy in her class. But talking to new people made her **nervous**. The thought of it made her **tremble**. Her hands got a little shaky. But the boy seemed nice. So Olivia decided to **approach** him during recess. He was drawing in a notebook. His art was really good! Olivia was **astonished** at how good it was. She said hello and told him she loved drawing too. The boy smiled **pleasantly**. He showed her more of his drawings. They were even better. In fact, they were **exceptional**. The boy **invited** Olivia to sit and draw with him. From that moment on, they were great friends.

1. to go closer to something __ __ __ __ __ __ (__) __
2. worried or a little scared __ __ __ __ (__) __ __
3. asked someone to join you __ (__) __ __ __ __ __
4. shake a little when scared or nervous (__) __ __ __ __ __ __
5. very surprised or amazed __ __ __ __ __ __ __ __ (__) __
6. really great or special __ (__) __ __ __ __ __ __ __ __ __
7. in a nice or friendly way __ __ __ __ __ __ __ (__) __ __

What type of clues did the word detective find?
Write the circled letter from each word in order to find out.

__ __ __ __ __ __ __

Name: ______________________ Date: ______________

Define and Draw

Each of the sentences below contains a nonsense word in bold. Use context clues to figure what each nonsense word means. Then write that meaning on the line and draw a picture of the scene.

1. The kitten was **zeagler**, so she hid under the couch when visitors came over. ______________________

2. Yusef shared his snacks with his friends at the soccer game because he was **degony**. ______________________

3. The new waterslide was **ritzpick**, with twists and drops that made us scream with excitement. ______________________

Name: ______________________ Date: ______________

Character Clues

The way a character acts, feels, and thinks shows what kind of person he or she is. Words that tell what a character is like are called *character traits.*

KEY WORDS

cooperative	fair	hardworking	honest
kind	responsible	thoughtful	trustworthy

Read the definitions. Then unscramble the letters to spell each word.

1. oryhsutwtrt ______________________ able to keep promises
2. dnik ______________________ is caring, helpful, or nice
3. radwhgorkin ______________________ does one's best
4. sporesenbli ______________________ takes care of duties
5. arif ______________________ treats people equally
6. nohtes ______________________ tells the truth
7. ocipetvorae ______________________ willing to work with others
8. gthfhlutou ______________________ kind and caring of others

Name: ______________________________ Date: ____________________

What Am I?

There are many words that can tell readers what traits a character has.

KEY WORDS

cooperative	**fair**	**hardworking**	**honest**
kind	**responsible**	**thoughtful**	**trustworthy**

Use the key words to answer the riddles below.

1. I help my friends when skies are gray.
   I do nice things to brighten their day. __ __ __ __ __ __ __ __ __ __
2. I follow the rules and take just my share.
   I treat everyone equally because I care. __ __ __ __
3. I tell the truth, because I can.
   Telling lies? I'm not a fan. __ __ __ __ __ __
4. I clean my room and feed my pet.
   Weekly chores? I won't forget! __ __ __ __ __ __ __ __ __ __ __
5. I do my best and give my all,
   on every task, big and small. __ __ __ __ __ __ __ __ __ __ __
6. I promise you with my pinky.
   Your secrets are safe with me. __ __ __ __ __ __ __ __ __ __ __
7. Being nice with what I say,
   I spread smiles every day. __ __ __ __
8. I work with others and lend a hand.
   I help and listen whenever I can. __ __ __ __ __ __ __ __ __ __ __

Name: ______________________________ **Date:** ________________

Feelings Tic-Tac-Toe

Just like people, characters can feel many different emotions. Naming them helps us understand the characters and the story.

Read the feeling words. Above each word, draw a picture of something that makes people feel that way. Then find three positive emotions in a row for tic-tac-toe.

loved	fearful	shy
sad	peaceful	excited
bored	angry	happy

Name: ______________________________ Date: ______________

Feelings Forecast

Use the key words to complete the sentences below.
You will use each word only once.

KEY WORDS

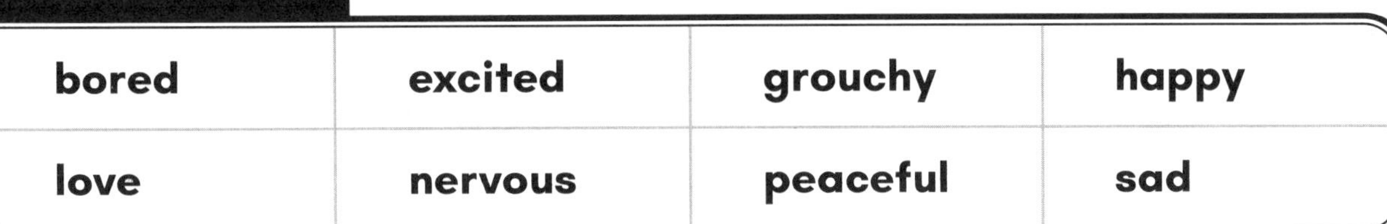

bored	excited	grouchy	happy
love	nervous	peaceful	sad

1. Madeline had nothing to do on a rainy Saturday. She was stuck inside.
   She was feeling ___ ___ ___ ___ ___ .
2. She was ___ (___) ___ that she and her friends couldn't play soccer.
3. Loud thunder always made Madeline (___) ___ ___ ___ ___ ___ ___ and jumpy.
4. When the power went out, she got more (___) ___ ___ ___ ___ ___ ___ .
5. Just then, her little brother asked, "Do you want to build a fort?"
   He was very ___ ___ (___) ___ ___ ___ ___ !
6. They made a cozy fort with blankets. Inside, it was quiet and very
   ___ ___ ___ ___ ___ ___ ___ ___ .
7. They used flashlights to read books together. Madeline smiled. She felt
   (___) ___ ___ ___ ___ .
8. "I ___ ___ ___ (___) rainy days now!" Madeline exclaimed.

How are feelings like the weather?
Unscramble the circled letters to find out.

Because they always ___ ___ ___ ___ ___ ___ .

Name: ______________________ Date: ______________

Mood Mates

Different words can have the same, or similar, meanings. These words are called *synonyms.*

Match each word about a feeling to its synonym.

1. lively

2. puzzled

3. furious

4. discouraged

5. calm

6. humiliated

7. envious

8. surprised

A.  embarrassed

B. confused

C. jealous

D.  disappointed

E.  energetic

F.  peaceful

G.  astonished

H.  angry

Name: ______________________ Date: ______________

Synonyms Soccer Score

Use the key word box to find a synonym for each bold word in the text below. Write the key word on the line. You will not use all the words.

KEY WORDS

angry	**calm**	**careful**
discouraged	**envious**	**humiliated**
puzzled	**shy**	**surprised**

Dear Liliana,

I had a big soccer game yesterday. Before the game, I felt ______________ (**1. relaxed**) and ready to play. In the last quarter, I ran toward the goal, hoping to score. I was ______________ (**2. astonished**) no one from the other team tried to stop me. I was also ______________ (**3. confused**). Why wasn't the other team being ______________ (**4. cautious**) to protect their goal? I kicked the ball hard and scored! That's when I saw the ______________ (**5. mad**) look on my coach's face. I'd kicked the ball into our own goal! I walked back to the sideline, head down and ______________ (**6. embarrassed**). My friend James ran over. I was ______________ (**7. jealous**) that he had scored a goal for our team earlier. "Sorry you're feeling down," he said. "You'll do better next time." James helped me feel less ______________ (**8. disappointed**). I hope you have a friend like James!

See you soon,

Andres

Name: ______________________________ **Date:** ______________

Same or Different Spinner

Some words mean the same thing. They are called *synonyms*. Some words mean the opposite of each other. They are called *antonyms*.

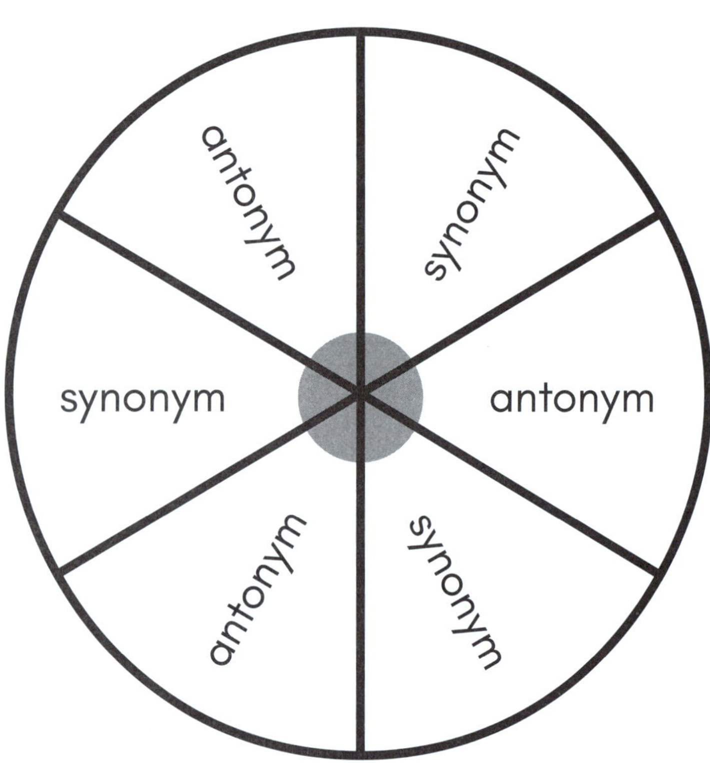

Place a pencil and a paper clip at the center of the spinner, as shown. Flick the paper clip to spin the spinner.

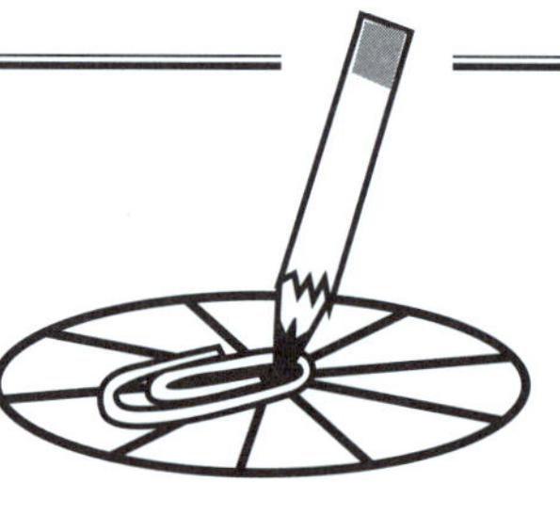

For each of the words below, spin the spinner. If it lands on *synonym*, circle S. Then write a word that means the same. If it lands on *antonym*, circle A. Then write a word that means the opposite.

1. bright	S / (A)	dark
2. happy	S / A	
3. cold	S / A	
4. fast	S / A	
5. big	S / A	
6. nice	S / A	
7. easy	S / A	

Name: ______________________ Date: ______________

What's the Opposite?

Write the correct key word next to its antonym.

KEY WORDS

empty	in	old	open
polite	push	slow	tall

1. young ______________
2. rude ______________
3. pull ______________
4. closed ______________
5. fast ______________
6. out ______________
7. short ______________
8. full ______________

What is a synonym for the word *antonym*?
Write the first letter of each of your answers in order to find out.

___ ___ ___ ___ ___ ___ ___ ___

Name: ____________________ Date: ____________

Prefix Power

A *base word* is a word that can stand on its own or combine with other word parts to make a new word. A *prefix* is a word part that goes at the beginning of a word.

Spin the wheel, then write the prefix next to a base word of your choice. If you make a real word, give yourself a point!

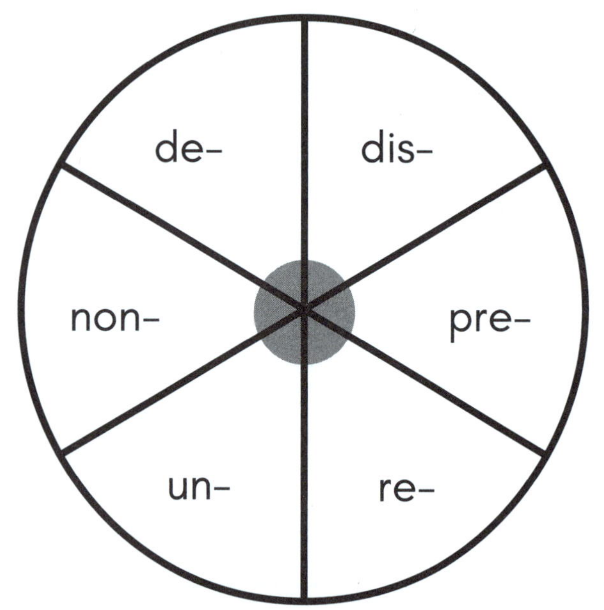

0-2 points: Prefix Explorer
3-5 points: Word Builder
6-7 points: Prefix Pro!

Place a pencil and a paper clip at the center of the spinner, as shown. Flick the paper clip to spin the spinner.

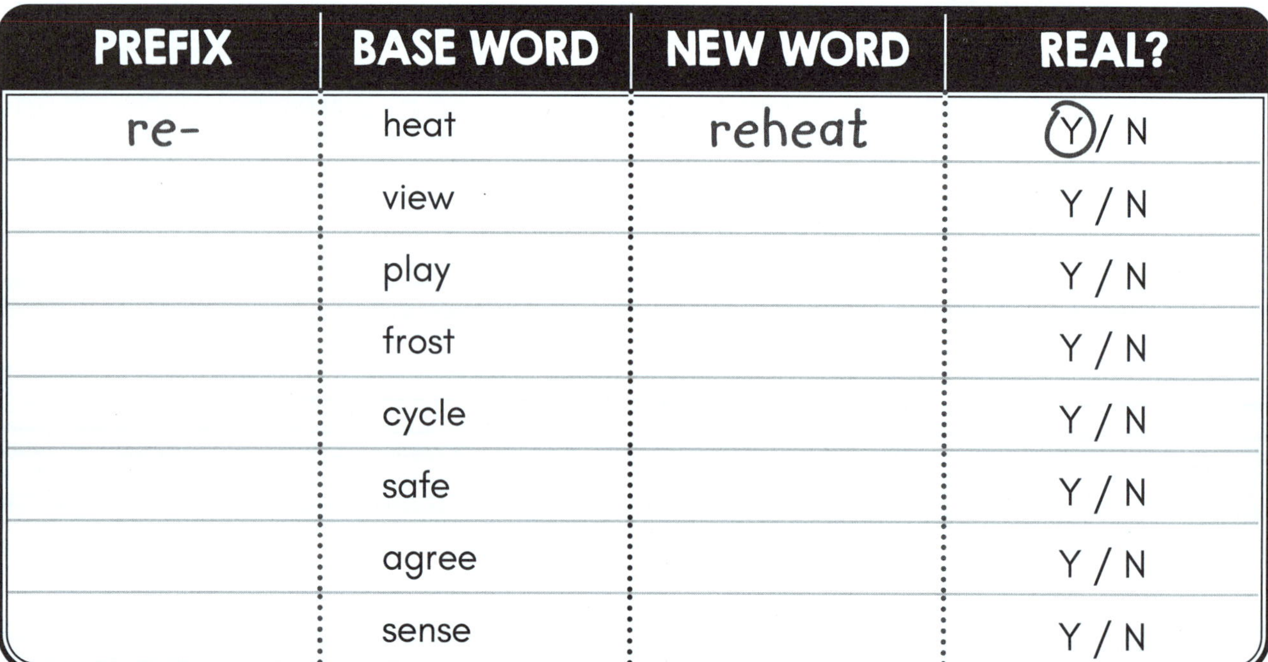

PREFIX	BASE WORD	NEW WORD	REAL?
re-	heat	reheat	(Y) / N
	view		Y / N
	play		Y / N
	frost		Y / N
	cycle		Y / N
	safe		Y / N
	agree		Y / N
	sense		Y / N

TOTAL ________

Name: ______________________ **Date:** ______________

Try Something New

Read the story. Circle the seven words that start with prefixes.

Dylan was excited to try snowboarding. The hill was big! It looked like nonstop fun. It also looked a bit scary. He readjusted his bag and previewed the safety rules.

Dylan didn't see his teacher, so he rechecked the map and reread his lesson ticket. He felt nervous and unsure. He wondered if he was in the wrong place.

"Dylan!" a cheerful voice called out. He turned to see his instructor walking up. She had a shiny snowboard under her arm. "We're going to have a great lesson! Don't feel discouraged. It can be tricky at first."

"Let's go!" he said with a smile.

Use one of the words you circled to answer the riddle.
What do you call a ski slope that never ends?

A  hill!

Name: ______________________________ **Date:** ________________

Bases Loaded

A *suffix* is a word part that is added to the end of a base word or root. Sometimes the new word will be a different part of speech than the base word.

KEY WORDS

brave	**bravely**	**bravery**
fast	**faster**	**fastest**
happy	**happiest**	**happiness**

Use the key words to complete the sentences below. You will use each word only once.

1. When I play with my best friend, I feel very ________________ .
2. It takes ________________ and courage to try something new.
3. Randa is the ________________ runner in our class.
4. I think firefighters are very ________________ because they run into fires.
5. My teacher solves math problems ________________ than I do.
6. My birthday is the ________________ day of the year for me.
7. Andy ________________ said he would go into the haunted house.
8. Shonda's big smile showed her ________________ about the good news.
9. Race cars go very ________________ around the track.

Name: ______________________ Date: ______________

Word Builder

Use the word parts below to build words. Score one point for each new word you make. Aim for 10 points.

WORDS	POINTS
action	1
TOTAL	

BASE WORDS

act	care
collect	color
danger	enjoy
help	skill
use	wonder

SUFFIXES

-able	-ed
-eous	-ful
-ible	-ion
-less	-ous

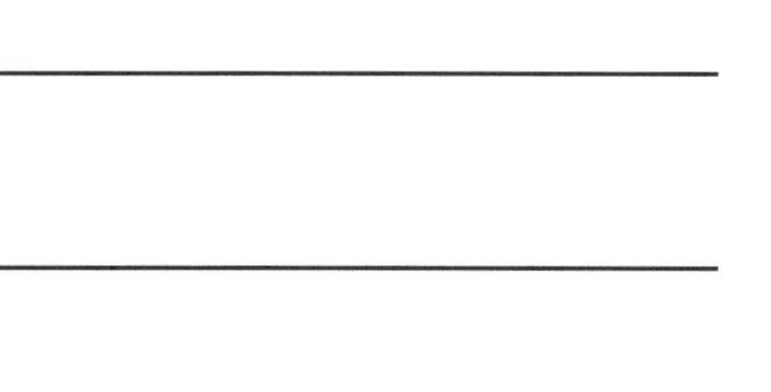

Name: ______________________ **Date:** ______________

Get to the Root of It

A *root* is the part of the word that carries the main meaning. Many English words have Latin roots. Knowing the meaning of these roots can help you understand words that contain them.

ROOT	MEANING	EXAMPLE
form	shape	*uniform*
port	to carry	*import*
scrib	to write	*scribe*

Match these words with Latin roots to their meanings.

1. uniform ●	● **A.** easy to carry
2. inform ●	● **B.** to give facts that shape what someone knows
3. import ●	● **C.** all the same in shape or look
4. scribe ●	● **D.** writing that is quick or messy
5. portable ●	● **E.** to carry something into a country
6. scribble ●	● **F.** a person who writes

Name: ______________________ Date: ______________

Ancient Word Architect

Use the word parts below to build words. Score one point for each word part you use. Aim for 10 points.

PREFIX	MEANING
com-/con-	with
de-	remove; reverse
re-	again

ROOT	MEANING
form	shape
port	to carry
scrib	to write

WORDS	POINTS
comport	2

TOTAL ______

Name: ______________________ **Date:** ______________

See and Hear

A *root* is the part of the word that carries the main meaning. Many science words are made from Latin roots. Knowing the meaning of these roots can help you understand words that contain them.

ROOT	MEANING	EXAMPLE
aud	to hear	*audio*
spec	to look	*inspect*
vis	to see	*vision*

Match these words with Latin roots to their meanings.

1. visible	**A.** to look closely
2. inspect	**B.** can be seen
3. audio	**C.** sound you can hear
4. spectacle	**D.** a beautiful view you can see
5. vista	**E.** to look up to someone
6. auditorium	**F.** something amazing to look at
7. respect	**G.** a large room where you hear concerts

Name: ______________________ **Date:** ______________

Looking for Words

The Latin roots *aud*, *spec*, and *vis* are used in many English words.

For each root, write as many words that use it as you can. Aim for five words for each one.

ROOT	MEANING	MY WORDS
aud	to hear	
spec	to look	
vis	to see	

Name: ______________________ **Date:** ______________

Riddle Me This, Scientist

The study of the natural world includes everything from tiny particles and living things on Earth to the stars and beyond.

KEY WORDS

gas	**gravity**	**liquid**	**orbit**
planet	**root**	**solid**	**stem**

Use the key words to answer the riddles below.

1. I keep you from floating out of sight.
I hold things on Earth down tight. ___ ___ ___ ___ ___ ___ ___

2. I stretch tall to reach the sun.
I hold up leaves, one by one. ___ ___ ___ ___

3. The air you breathe or bubbles clear,
I fill any space, far or near! ___ ___ ___

4. Deep in the soil is where I hide.
Collecting water to store inside. ___ ___ ___ ___

5. I have a shape that rarely bends.
Unlike liquid and gas, my two friends. ___ ___ ___ ___ ___

6. I go round and round the sun.
Of the eight, I'm only one. ___ ___ ___ ___ ___ ___

7. I pour from cups hot and cold.
I'm wet, I flow, and I'm hard to hold. ___ ___ ___ ___ ___ ___

8. I'm the path a planet makes,
looping around in outer space. ___ ___ ___ ___ ___

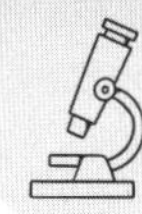

Name: ______________________ **Date:** ______________

Sorting Science

Think about how the words below connect to one another. Create three groups of three related words by coloring each group red, yellow, or blue.

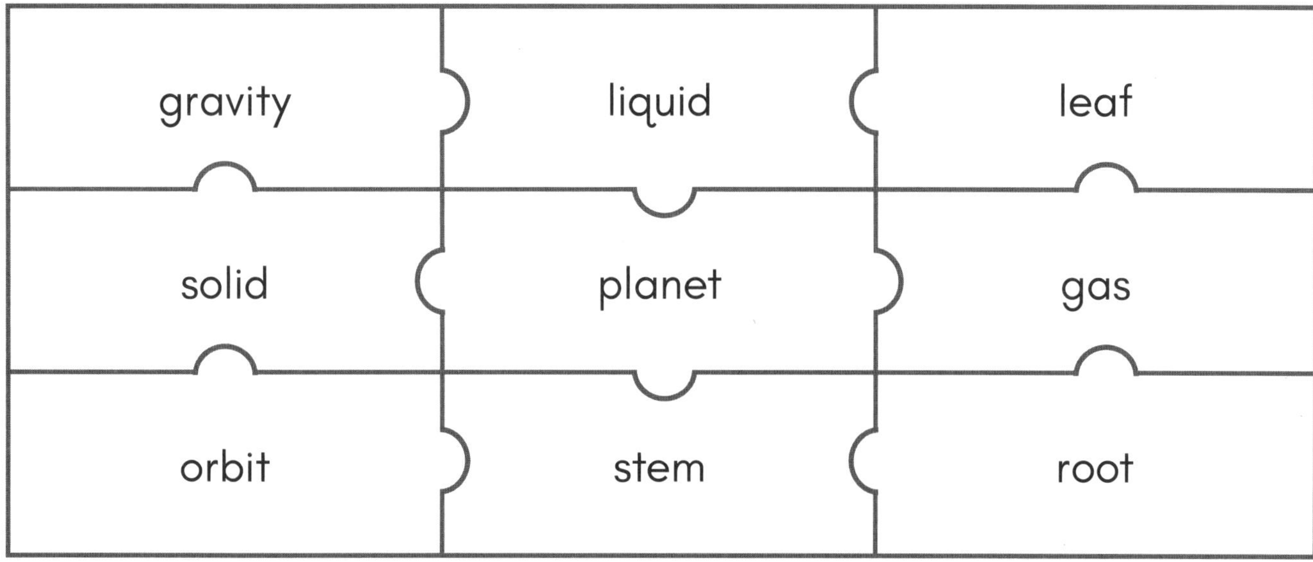

Explain what the words in each group have in common.

RED GROUP ______________________

____

YELLOW GROUP ______________________

____

BLUE GROUP ______________________

____

Name: ______________________ Date: ______________

What Do Scientists Do?

Scientists learn, explore, and solve problems. They use their skills to make new discoveries, invent things, and answer important questions.

Read each key word and its meaning.

KEY WORDS

★ **classify**	sort things into groups
★ **design**	plan and create something
★ **invent**	create something new
★ **investigate**	examine something closely
★ **model**	show how something works
★ **observe**	watch carefully
★ **predict**	make a guess about what will happen
★ **research**	study and gather information

Think about a time you acted like a scientist. Write about it below. Use at least two of the key words.

____

____

____

Name: ______________________ Date: ______________

Science Search & Spell

Find the key science words in the puzzle. Words can go → or ↓.

WORD BANK

classify	design	invent	investigate
model	observe	predict	research

d	e	s	i	g	n	r	a	o	o
u	m	n	c	p	i	e	c	d	b
k	o	q	l	r	n	y	p	a	s
a	d	a	a	e	v	o	g	w	e
b	e	d	s	d	e	n	p	p	r
i	l	m	s	i	s	s	s	v	v
n	b	w	i	c	t	t	e	n	e
v	o	l	f	t	i	g	w	u	i
e	c	w	y	f	g	a	r	x	g
n	a	g	o	a	a	t	f	y	l
t	f	k	h	p	t	e	n	i	r
z	e	r	e	s	e	a	r	c	h

Name: ______________________ Date: ______________

Who Studies What?

Some science words end in the suffix -*ology*, which means "the study of." When we add the suffix -*ist* to a word, it means "a person who studies" that topic.

Look at the key words in the box. Drop the -*y* at the end of each word. Add -*ist* to make the name of a scientist. Then fill in the blanks to tell what that type of scientist studies.

KEY WORDS

botany	ecology	geology
meteorology	paleontology	zoology

	SCIENTIST NAME	WHAT THEY STUDY
1.	botanist	plants
2.		
3.		
4.		
5.		
6.		

Name: ______________________ Date: ______________

Scientist Self-Portrait

Choose a type of scientist. Draw a picture of yourself doing that job. Be sure to include the tools you would use for your job and label them.

Write a sentence about why you chose this type of scientist.

Name: ______________________ Date: ______________

Home Sweet Habitat

Every animal needs a *habitat*, a place to live. From freezing climates to sunny deserts, there are many different types of habitats. Each one provides the food, water, and shelter that animals need to survive.

KEY WORDS

freshwater	grassland	mountaintop	riverbank
seashore	wetland	woodland	☆ ☆

Read the definitions. Then unscramble the letters to spell each word.

1. wraesrfeth ______________________ a non-salty body of water
2. sgladrsan ______________________ an area covered with grasses
3. orashsee ______________________ the land next to the ocean
4. tndewal ______________________ a swamp or marsh
5. knarevirb ______________________ the land next to a stream
6. tpmotainuon ______________________ the peak of a very tall landform
7. dadowoln ______________________ an area with many trees

Each of the words above is made up of two other words. For example, *freshwater = fresh + water*. What do we call these kinds of words?

____

Name: ______________________ Date: ______________

Building Good Habitats

One letter is missing from each wheel below. Figure out where each word starts. Then add one key letter to complete it.

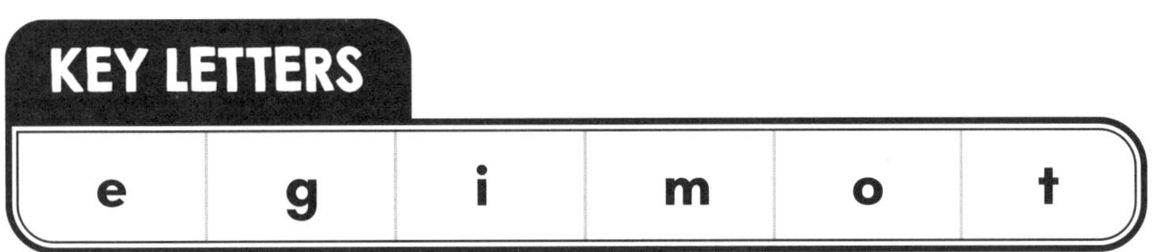

1.

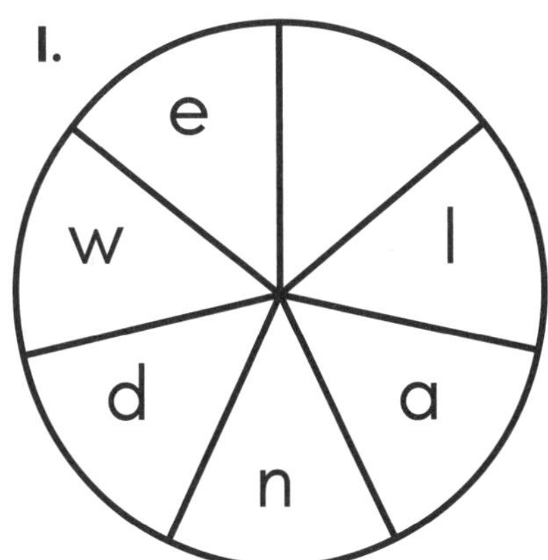

2.

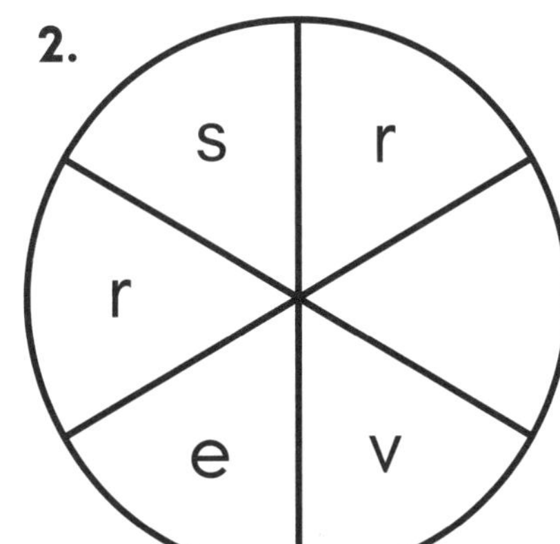

3.

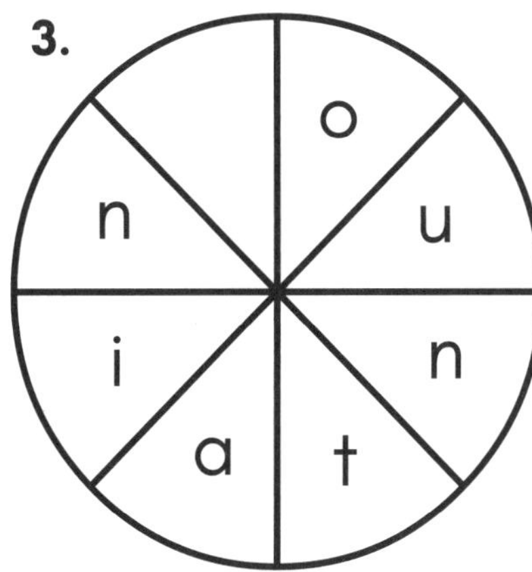

4.

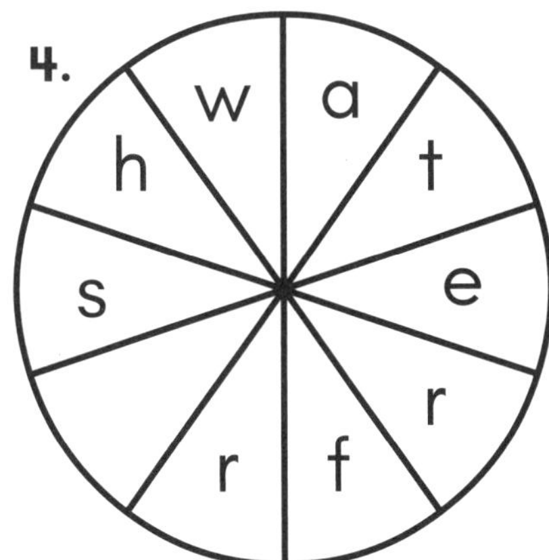

5.

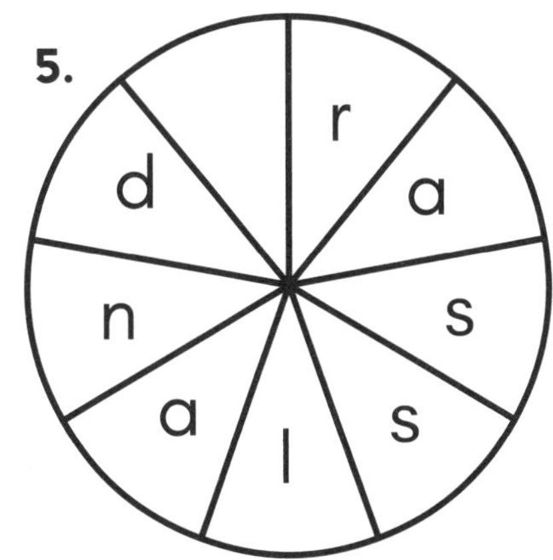

6.

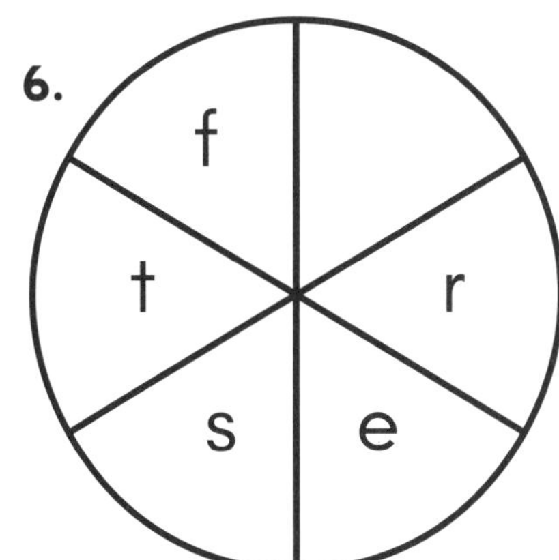

What time is it when you see a lion walk onto the savanna? Write the missing letters in order to find out.

____ ____ ____ ____ to ____ ____!

Name: ______________________ Date: ______________

What Comes Next?

Living things grow and change. Plants and animals go through different stages as they develop into adults.

Use the key words to fill in the puzzle. Letters are shared when the words cross.

KEY WORDS
adult
larva
metamorphosis
offspring
pupa
reproduce
seed
sprout

ACROSS

2. The part of a plant that can grow into a new plant

4. To have children or grow new plants

6. The fully grown stage of a plant or an animal

7. A big change in an animal's form as it grows

DOWN

1. A caterpillar or other wormlike young form of an insect

2. A new plant that has just started growing

3. The life stage when an insect changes inside a shell or case

5. The babies of an animal

Name: ____________________ Date: ____________

Round and Round

Think about how the words below connect to one another. Create three groups of three related words by coloring each group red, yellow, or blue.

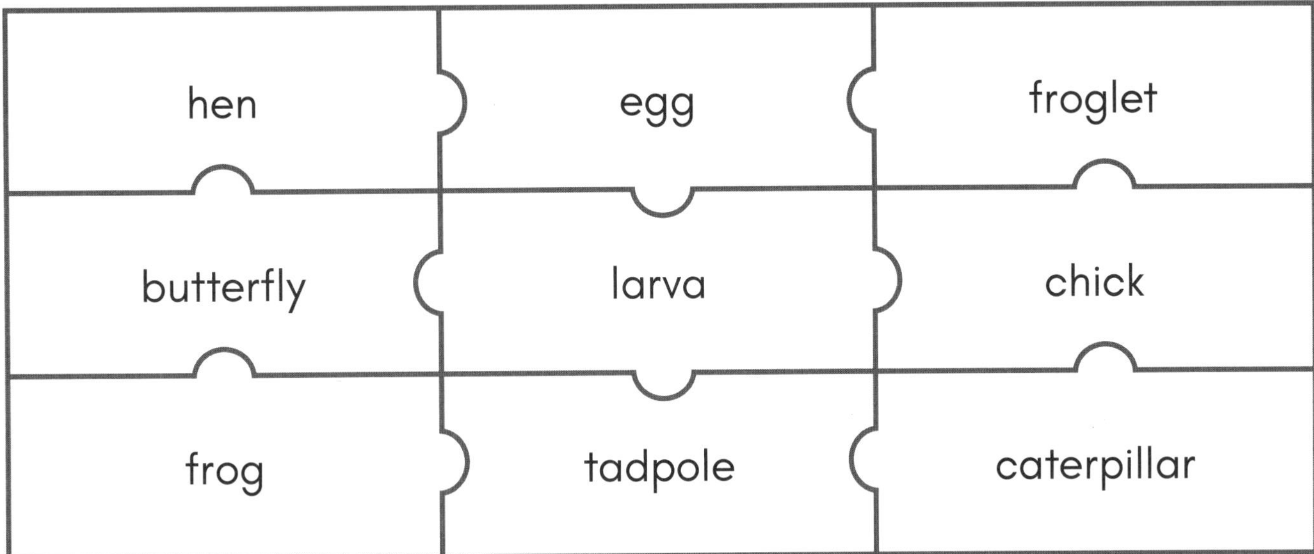

Explain what the words in each group have in common.

RED GROUP ____________________

____

YELLOW GROUP ____________________

____

BLUE GROUP ____________________

____

Name: ______________________ **Date:** ______________

Trait Tracker

Traits can be inherited from parents or learned over time. An *adaptation* is a trait that helps a plant or animal survive in its environment.

KEY WORDS

adapt	**behavior**	**camouflage**	**habitat**
inherit	**mimicry**	**survive**	**traits**

Use the key words to complete the sentences below.
You will use each word only once.

1. Many traits help animals live, or (__) __ __ __ __ __ __ .
2. Some animals use __ __ __ __ (__) __ __ __ __ __ , colors or patterns that help them blend into their surroundings.
3. The place an animal lives is called its __ (__) __ __ __ __ __ .
4. An animal's __ (__) __ __ __ __ __ __ is the way it acts.
5. If the environment changes, animals may also need to change, or __ __ __ __ (__) , to survive.
6. Some animals pretend to be another animal to fool predators! This clever trick is called __ __ __ __ (__) __ __ .
7. The physical __ __ __ __ __ (__) of an animal, such as its tail, teeth, or fins, can help it survive.
8. Animals (__) __ __ __ __ __ __ some traits from their parents.

Why do elephants have trunks?
Unscramble the circled letters to find out.

Because they don't have s __ __ __ __ __ __ __ __ .

Name: ______________________ Date: ______________

How Can Animals Thrive?

Find the key words about traits and adaptations in the puzzle. Words can go → or ↓.

WORD BANK

adapt	behavior	camouflage	habitat
inherit	mimicry	survive	trait

m	e	j	a	s	t	r	a	i	t
w	u	j	g	f	x	d	c	d	g
r	c	l	l	m	z	i	a	i	r
b	e	q	p	v	e	k	m	n	q
e	o	p	m	i	s	o	o	h	l
h	v	w	i	h	u	b	u	e	x
a	n	t	m	a	r	a	f	r	t
v	r	i	i	b	v	u	l	i	g
i	s	u	c	i	i	g	a	t	r
o	u	i	r	t	v	l	g	d	u
r	m	j	y	a	e	l	e	e	e
a	d	a	p	t	g	a	z	t	j

Name: ______________________ **Date:** ______________

Ready, Set, Motion!

Things move when they are pushed or pulled. The harder you push or pull something, the faster or farther it can go.

KEY WORDS

accelerate	**direction**	**force**	**friction**
gravity	**motion**	**position**	**speed**

Read the definitions. Then unscramble the letters to spell each word.

1. ptonisio ______________ where something is located
2. cirofnit ______________ the rubbing of one object against another that slows objects down
3. aivyrtg ______________ the force that pulls things toward the center of the Earth
4. tocerindi ______________ the way that something is moving, such as left or north
5. elarecatce ______________ to move faster and faster
6. oitnom ______________ the movement of something from one place to another
7. pesde ______________ how fast something is moving
8. coerf ______________ an action that makes something move, change direction, or stop moving

Name: ______________________ **Date:** ______________

Force and Motion Commotion

Look at each set of words. Think about what the words have in common. Then circle the word in each set that does not belong. Explain your reasoning.

1. push, pull, run, twist	**2.** float, grow, sink, slide
Explain: ______________	**Explain:** ______________
3. ramp, lever, planet, pulley	**4.** color, direction, fast, slow
Explain: ______________	**Explain:** ______________

Name: ______________________ **Date:** ______________

Magnetic Mix-Up

Magnets can pull certain metals, such as iron, toward them. Every magnet has two ends called *poles*. One is north and one is south. The north pole of one magnet will pull toward the south pole of another. Two north poles will push apart, or *repel*. Two south poles will also repel.

KEY WORDS

attract	**compass**	**field**	**magnet**
north	**pole**	**repel**	**south**

Read the definitions. Then unscramble the letters to spell each word.

1. ohrtn ______________ a magnet's end that points to the North Pole
2. lerpe ______________ what magnets do when they push away
3. thuso ______________ the pole of a magnet that repels the south pole of another
4. tartcat ______________ what magnets do when they pull
5. elpo ______________ another word for the end of a magnet
6. gamten ______________ a material that attracts iron
7. sampcos ______________ a tool with a magnetic needle that points north
8. delif ______________ the area around a magnet

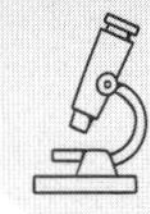

Name: ______________________ Date: ______________

Opposites Attract

Find the key words about magnets in the puzzle. Words can go → or ↓.

WORD BANK

attract	compass	field	magnet
north	pole	repel	south

t	s	m	a	g	n	e	t	q	u
c	z	u	e	r	t	q	n	o	q
a	f	i	e	l	d	l	u	z	s
t	o	g	r	n	c	g	d	s	n
t	b	r	u	d	o	l	a	f	o
r	j	m	c	c	m	d	n	s	r
a	u	t	r	e	p	e	l	s	t
c	c	p	n	u	a	a	v	o	h
t	h	o	o	c	s	v	l	u	w
y	f	t	f	r	s	f	c	t	o
h	g	z	a	e	e	u	a	h	p
c	p	o	l	e	u	m	q	v	x

Name: ________________________________ **Date:** ________________

What's the Matter?

Matter is anything that has mass and takes up space. Matter can be in different forms, or *states*. It can be a solid, liquid, or gas. Matter can even change from one state to another.

Use the key words to fill in the puzzle. Letters are shared when the words cross.

KEY WORDS
boil
condensation
evaporation
freeze
melt
precipitation
vapor
water cycle

ACROSS

5. Water that falls from the sky

6. When heat makes a solid turn into a liquid

7. When water gets hot and starts to bubble

8. When water turns into gas and rises up

DOWN

1. Water in the air that you can't see

2. The path water moves on, above, and below the earth's surface

3. When water vapor turns into drops of water

4. When water turns into ice

Name: ______________________ Date: ______________

Solid, Liquid, or Gas?

What did the cloud say to the water vapor? Use the Code Breaker Key to find out.

CODE BREAKER KEY

A	B	C	D	E	F	G	H	I	J	K	L	M
N	O	P	Q	R	S	T	U	V	W	X	Y	Z

Name: ______________________________ Date: ________________

A Bone to Pick

Millions of years ago, dinosaurs and other creatures roamed our planet. Today, scientists called *paleontologists* study their remains to learn about these prehistoric animals and what their lives might have been like.

KEY WORDS

amber	**bones**	**extinct**
fossil	**sediment**	**skeleton**

Read the definitions. Then unscramble the letters to spell each word.

1. sofils ____________________ remains or imprints of plants and animals from long ago
2. centxit ____________________ gone forever, like dinosaurs
3. beson ____________________ parts of a skeleton
4. bearm ____________________ sticky tree sap that can harden and preserve plants or animals
5. esolkten ____________________ all the bones in a body that give it shape and support
6. minesedt ____________________ small pieces of rock, sand, or dirt

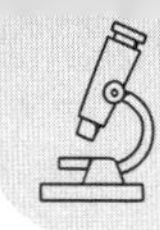

Name: ______________________ **Date:** ______________

Dig Into the Past

Scientists dig deeply and carefully into the earth to find clues about prehistoric plants and animals.

KEY WORDS

amber	**bones**	**extinct**
fossil	**sediment**	**skeleton**

Use the key words to answer the riddles below.

1. I trapped a juicy bug and turned gold.
   I'm glossy, hard, and very old. ___ ___ ___ ___ ___

2. I was once alive, long, long ago.
   Beneath the earth I now lie low. ___ ___ ___ ___ ___ ___

3. Bits of mud, sand, and clay
   that settle slowly day by day. ___ ___ ___ ___ ___ ___ ___ ___

4. Made of bones from head to toe,
   I help you stand and help you grow. ___ ___ ___ ___ ___ ___ ___ ___

5. I'm no longer alive,
   though I once used to be.
   There are only traces
   or bones left of me. ___ ___ ___ ___ ___ ___ ___

6. Hard, strong, and inside you—
   dinosaurs had them too! ___ ___ ___ ___ ___

Name: ______________________________ **Date:** ____________________

Rock On!

There are three main types of rocks. *Igneous* rocks are made when melted rock, like lava or magma, cools and hardens. Examples include basalt and granite. *Sedimentary* rocks are made from bits of sand, shells, or other materials that pile up in layers and harden over time. Limestone and sandstone are this type of rock. *Metamorphic* rocks begin as other rock types, but heat and pressure deep inside the Earth change them. Marble and slate are metamorphic rocks.

Use the letters in the word below to make as many other words as you can. Give yourself one point for each three-letter word, two points for each four-letter word, and three points for any longer words.

sedimentary

WORDS	POINTS	WORDS	POINTS

TOTAL ________

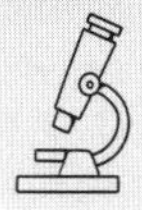

Name: ______________________ Date: ______________

Climb the Rock Ladder

Climb the word ladder to change *shale* into another word that relates to rocks. Read each clue and follow the directions to create a new word.

A small rock or pebble.

7. ___ ___ ___ ___ ___

Change one letter.

What the sun did yesterday.

6. ___ ___ ___ ___ ___

Change one letter.

Where land meets water at a beach.

5. ___ ___ ___ ___ ___

Change one letter.

Make a point in a game.

4. ___ ___ ___ ___ ___

Change one letter.

To make someone feel afraid.

3. ___ ___ ___ ___ ___

Change one letter.

A small, flat piece of hard skin on fish.

2. ___ ___ ___ ___ ___

Change one letter.

1. s h a l e

Name: ______________________________ Date: ________________

Weather Wise

Weather can change every day—from peaceful skies to powerful storms. Learning about different weather events helps us stay safe and know what to do during emergencies.

Use the key words to fill in the puzzle. Letters are shared when the words cross.

KEY WORDS

- drought
- emergency
- flood
- forecast
- hail
- shelter
- snow
- tornado
- weather

ACROSS

1. A safe place, or _____, is important to have during dangerous weather.
2. Water that covers land, maybe due to a very heavy rain
5. Practice drills help people know what to do in an _____.
6. Pea- or softball-sized balls of ice that fall from the sky
7. Strong winds that twist into a funnel shape over land

DOWN

1. Fluffy, white frozen water in winter
2. A _____ tells people what kind of weather to expect.
3. When there's no rain for a long time and the land gets very dry
4. Stormy, sunny, rainy, and snowy are all different kinds of _____.

Name: ______________________ **Date:** ______________

Natural Forces

Use the Code Breaker Key to solve the puzzle and reveal a saying about the weather.

CODE BREAKER KEY

A	B	C	D	E	F	G	H	I	J	K	L	M
N	**O**	**P**	**Q**	**R**	**S**	**T**	**U**	**V**	**W**	**X**	**Y**	**Z**

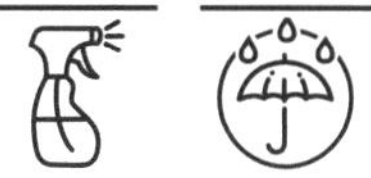        

    ,       .

Name: ______________________________ **Date:** ______________

Pick a Precipitation

The water cycle shows how water moves in and around Earth. *Precipitation* is the stage of the water cycle in which water falls from the sky.

KEY WORDS

clouds	**crystals**	**droplets**	**hail**
rain	**sleet**	**snowflakes**	**vapor**

Use the key words to complete the sentences below.
You will use each word only once.

1. Another name for water in gas form is water ________________.
2. When air cools, small ________________ of water may begin to form in the sky.
3. Water vapor can also cool into tiny ice ________________.
4. ________________ are made of many water droplets or ice crystals floating in the air.
5. When ________________ falls, it might come down as a light drizzle or a dangerous downpour.
6. In cold climates, unique hexagons of ice called ________________ form in freezing air.
7. If snow meets warmer air as it falls, it forms frozen rain called ________________.
8. During a thunderstorm, balls of frozen water called ________________ might fall.

Name: ______________________________ Date: ________________

Climb the Precipitation Ladder

Climb the word ladder to change *rain* into another word that relates to precipitation. Read each clue and follow the directions to create a new word.

7. ___ ___ ___ ___ ← Frozen balls of ice that fall from the sky.

Change one letter.

What a dog wags. → 6. ___ ___ ___ ___

Change one letter.

5. ___ ___ ___ ___ ← What you hit with a hammer.

Change one letter.

Envelopes delivered to your home. → 4. ___ ___ ___ ___

Change one letter.

3. ___ ___ ___ ___ ← The most important idea in a text.

Change one letter.

To get more of something. → 2. ___ ___ ___ ___

Change one letter.

1. **r a i n**

Name: ______________________ Date: ______________

The Three R's

Conservation is using Earth's resources wisely so they last a long time. Learning the three R's—reduce, reuse, and recycle—is a great way to start making a difference.

Use the key words to fill in the puzzle.
Letters are shared when the words cross.

KEY WORDS

- cleanup
- environment
- garbage
- landfill
- pollution
- recycle
- reduce
- reuse

ACROSS

4. Things we throw in the trash
5. To make less waste
7. Harmful waste, such as smog or litter

DOWN

1. The natural world around us
2. A place where trash is taken
3. To use something again
5. To take something used or old and turn it into something new that can be used again
6. The removal of trash

Name: ______________________ Date: ______________

Planet Protectors

How can you help Earth?
Use the Code Breaker Key to find out.

CODE BREAKER KEY

A	B	C	D	E	F	G	H	I	J	K	L	M
N	**O**	**P**	**Q**	**R**	**S**	**T**	**U**	**V**	**W**	**X**	**Y**	**Z**

____ ____ ____ ____ ____ ____ ,

____ ____ ____ ____ ____ , ____ ____ ____

____ ____ ____ ____ ____ ____ ____ .

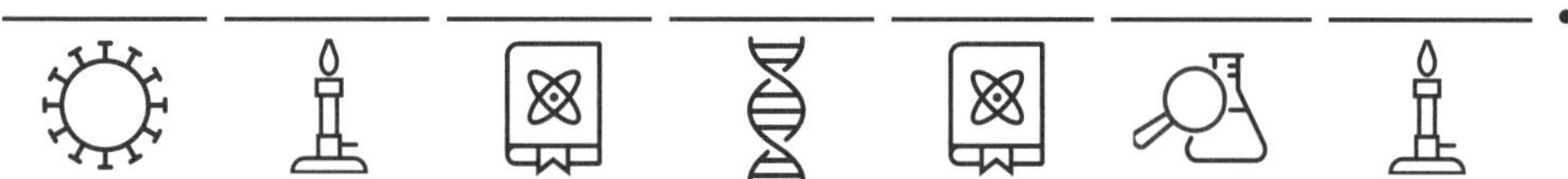

Name: ______________________________ **Date:** ____________________

Money Talks

A *root* is the part of the word that carries the main meaning. Many social studies words have Latin roots. Knowing the meaning of Latin roots can help you understand words that contain them.

LATIN ROOT	MEANING	EXAMPLE
duce/duct	to lead or bring	*conduct*
mand	to order or ask	*command*
port	to carry	*import*
tract	to pull or drag	*tractor*

Match these words with Latin roots to their meanings.

1. produce ●	● **A.** to direct or lead a band
2. tractor ●	● **B.** to carry something into a country
3. import ●	● **C.** to make or bring something
4. demand ●	● **D.** to order someone to do something
5. conduct ●	● **E.** to strongly ask for something
6. command ●	● **F.** a farm vehicle that pulls a wagon

Name: ______________________ Date: ______________

The Root Cause

Use the word parts below to build words. Give yourself one point for each word part you use. Aim for 10 points.

PREFIX	MEANING
de-	down
ex-	out; away
in-	into
pro-	before; forward

ROOT	MEANING
duce/duct	to lead or bring
mand	to order or ask
port	to carry
tract	to pull or drag

WORDS	POINTS
deduce	2

TOTAL ______

Name: ______________________ **Date:** ____________

Community Belongings

A *community* is a place where people live, work, and play together. A community can be any size, from a big city to your classroom!

Look at each set of words. Think about what the words have in common. Then circle the word in each set that does not belong. Explain your reasoning.

1. principal, teacher, firefighter, custodian

Explain: ______________________

____

____

____

____

2. family, boat, team, neighbors

Explain: ______________________

____

____

____

____

3. volunteer, celebrate, gather, fly

Explain: ______________________

____

____

____

____

4. zip code, street, river, city

Explain: ______________________

____

____

____

____

Name: ______________________ Date: ____________

It Takes a Village

Communities are made up of people who do different kinds of jobs. Every person helps keep the community strong.

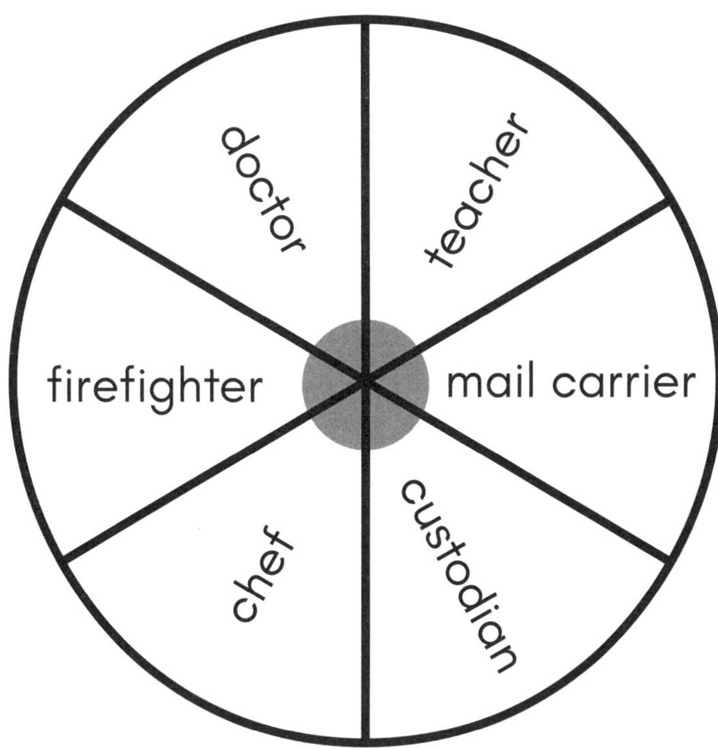

Place a pencil and a paper clip at the center of the spinner, as shown. Flick the paper clip to spin the spinner.

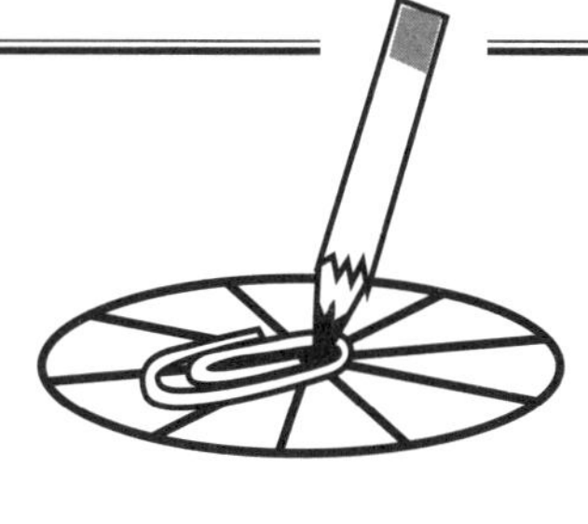

Spin the wheel. Circle the job it lands on. Then use that job to answer the questions.

1. Where does this person work? ____________
2. What tools do they use? ____________
3. How do they help people? ____________
4. What might happen if they didn't do their job? ____________
5. Would you like to do this job? Why or why not? ____________

Name: ______________________ **Date:** ______________

It's Your Right

A *right* is something everyone deserves, like being treated fairly or having enough food. A *responsibility* is something you're expected to do, like chores and homework. We all have both!

Help the pirates get to the treasure chest. Draw a line by following the rights. Don't go through the responsibilities. They're traps!

Voting in elections	Following classroom rules	Listening to others	Speaking kindly
Speaking freely	Being treated fairly	Wearing a bicycle helmet	Cooperating with your peers
Respecting others' property	Having access to food	Making healthy food choices	Doing your homework
Helping keep your space clean	Getting help in emergencies	Drinking clean water	Walking your dog
Taking turns	Brushing teeth	Being safe	Practicing your religion

Name: ______________________ Date: ______________

Doing What's Right

Find the key word that completes each sentence below. Write it in the spaces provided. Each new word begins with the last letter of the word before it.

KEY WORDS

effort	**equal**	**kindness**	**leader**	**respect**
rule	**safety**	**share**	**task**	**tools**

1. Each day, Mr. McGee goes over a class r u l e to help us stay safe and play fairly.
2. Everyone should have an e ___ ___ ___ ___ chance to speak, play, and learn.
3. Today I was line ___ ___ ___ ___ ___ ___, so I was in the front.
4. I showed ___ ___ ___ ___ ___ ___ ___ by walking quietly and slowly.
5. When it was time to clean up, my ___ ___ ___ ___ was to stack chairs.
6. I showed ___ ___ ___ ___ ___ ___ ___ ___ by helping Amie when she dropped her supplies.
7. I told her we could ___ ___ ___ ___ ___ my crayons.
8. Even though science was hard, I gave my best ___ ___ ___ ___ ___ ___.
9. We used ___ ___ ___ ___ ___ to complete the experiment.
10. Rules about ___ ___ ___ ___ ___ ___ in the science lab help keep us from getting hurt.

Name: ______________________ Date: ______________

What Do I Need?

Everyone has things they need to survive, such as air to breathe. Other things we just want for fun, such as games. Knowing the difference between needs and wants helps us take care of the most important things first.

KEY WORDS

bicycle	**camera**	**food**
phone	**safety**	**shelter**
toys	**truck**	**water**

Write each key word in the correct column, depending on whether it is something people need or something they might want.

NEEDS	WANTS

BONUS **Add more examples of needs and wants to the lists above.**

Name: ______________________________ Date: ____________________

What Do I Want?

One letter is missing from each wheel below. Figure out where each word starts. Then add one key letter to complete it.

KEY LETTERS

c	d	e	e	h	l	o	r

1.
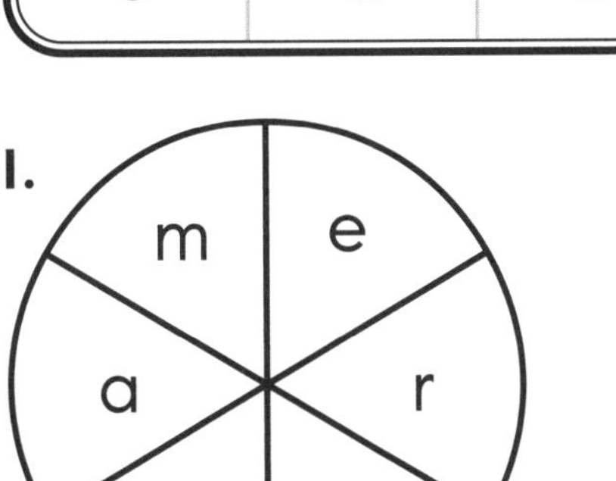

2.
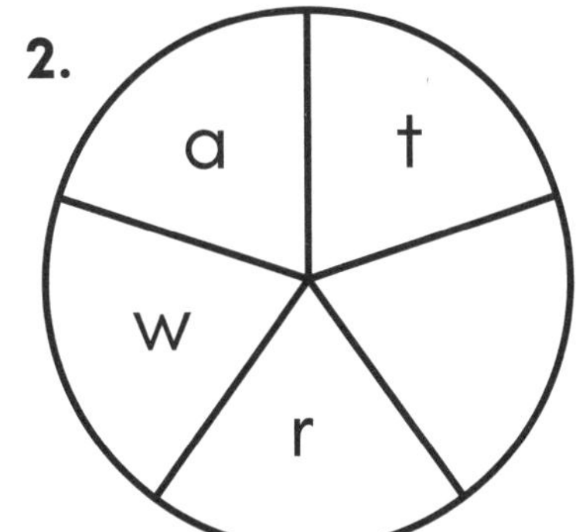

3.
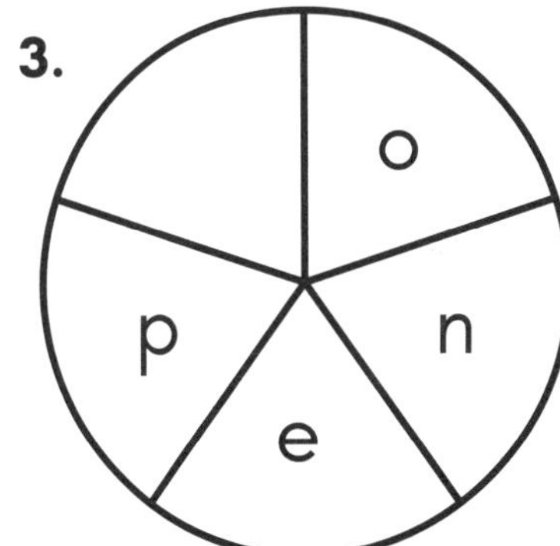

4.
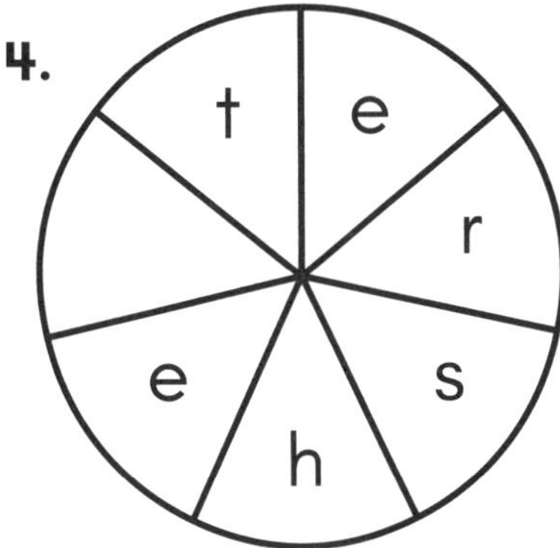

5.
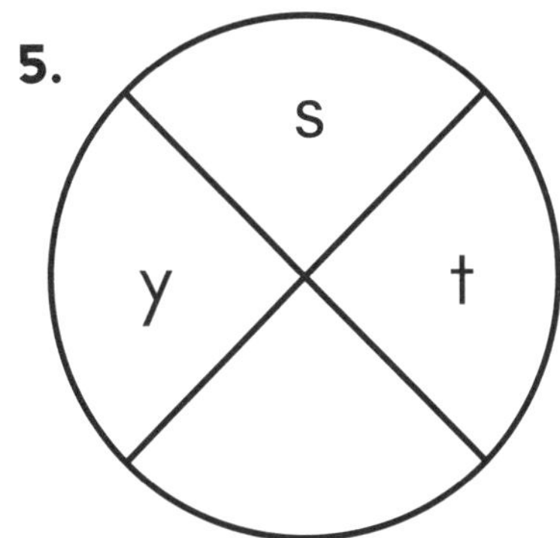

6.
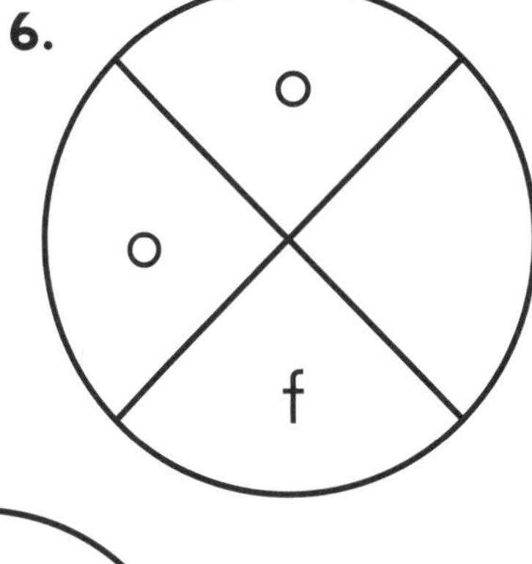

7.
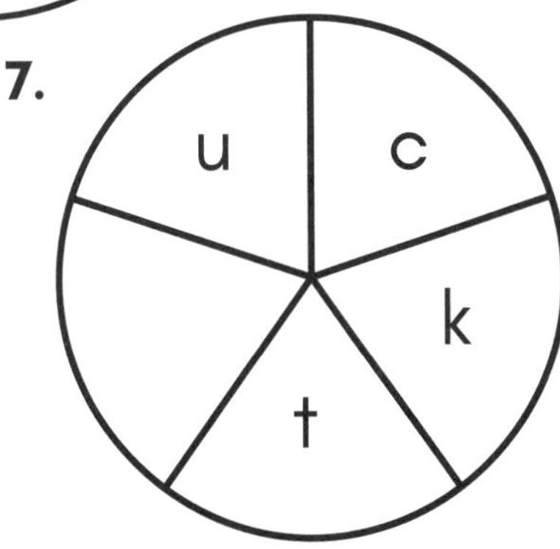

8.
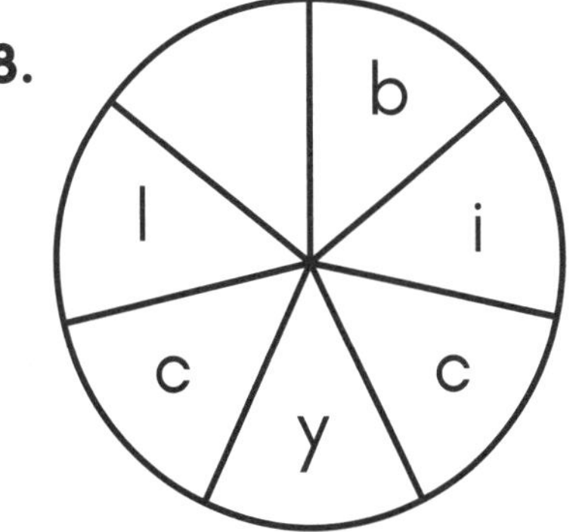

Circle the words that are wants. Write their missing letters in order to find the word for a task you have to do.

___ ___ ___ ___ ___

Name: ______________________ Date: ______________

Good Service

People buy goods, like food or clothes, online or in stores. People also buy services, such as seeing a doctor or getting a car repaired.

KEY WORDS

consumer	earn	economy	goods
money	producer	service	supply

Read the definitions. Then unscramble the letters to spell each word.

1. dogos ______________ something you can buy or use, like a toy or a backpack
2. ncomuser ______________ the person who buys a good or service
3. cedruorp ______________ the person who makes a good or does a service
4. spylup ______________ the amount of products a store has available to sell
5. moneyoc ______________ a country's system of buying and selling things
6. nrea ______________ to get something by working for it
7. oymen ______________ coins or paper bills used to buy things
8. erseicv ______________ work someone does for someone else

Name: ______________________ Date: ______________

It's All Good(s)

Find the key words about the goods and services in the puzzle. Words can go → or ↓.

WORD BANK

consumer	earn	economy	goods
money	producer	service	supply

b	g	s	o	s	u	h	c	y
x	y	u	o	e	a	r	n	s
u	p	p	d	q	c	n	h	e
c	r	p	c	v	x	p	i	r
o	o	l	g	o	o	d	s	v
n	d	y	d	m	f	w	t	i
s	u	d	s	o	g	a	a	c
u	c	j	m	n	g	g	e	e
m	e	e	k	e	h	s	e	a
e	r	q	j	y	p	d	m	w
r	e	c	o	n	o	m	y	n

Name: ______________________ Date: ______________

Travel Twisters

People and goods travel in many different ways, such as by land, water, and air.

The letters of the words below have been scrambled. Unscramble each word. Use the pictures to help.

1. krtuc 

2.  nitra 

3.  emloctyocr 

4.  rapainle 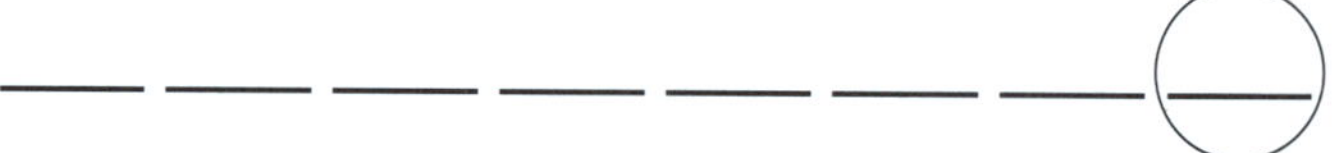

5.  rryef 

6. 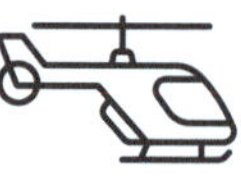 cthrpeiloe 

7.  phis 

8.  cehvile 

9.  sub ___ ___ ___

What happens when you wear a watch on an airplane? Write the circled letters in order to find out.

___ ___ ___ ___   ___ ___ ___ ___ ___ !

Name: ______________________ Date: ______________

Let's Move!

Climb the word ladder to change *bike* into another word that relates to transportation. Read each clue and follow the directions to create a new word.

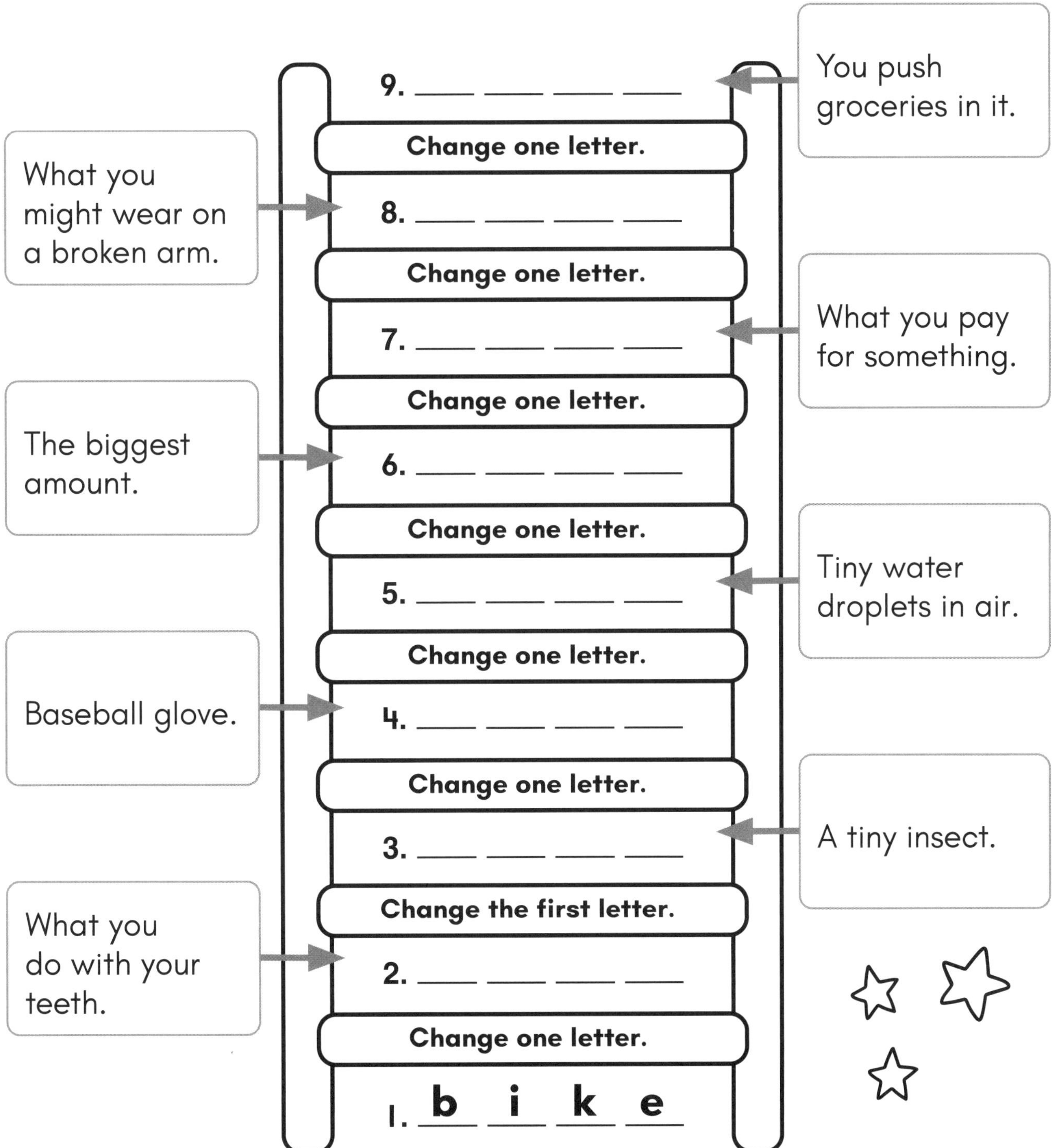

Name: ______________________________ Date: ______________

Map Mix-Up

Maps help us understand the world around us. They show distances, borders, and important places. Knowing how to read maps makes exploring new places easier and more fun.

Unscramble each word about maps to complete the sentences below.

1. A ______________ is a map of the Earth in the shape of a sphere.
   lobge

2. Horizontal lines on a globe show ______________, and vertical lines show longitude.
   taitdelu

3. You use a compass ______________ to find north on a map.
   seor

4. The Earth has two ______________, one in the north and one in the south.
   solpe

5. If a map says one inch equals one mile, that is the ______________ .
   csela

6. The ______________ is an imaginary line that goes around the middle of the Earth.
   raoqute

7. Some lines on a map show the ______________ between countries.
   drbseor

8. North, south, east, and west are the ______________ directions.
   inadlrca

9. A map's ______________ contains symbols that can help you identify geographic features.
   eyk

10. Distances on maps are measured in ______________ or kilometers.
    liems

Name: ______________________ Date: ______________

Odd Map Out

Look at each set of words. Think about what the words have in common. Then circle the word in each set that does not belong. Explain your reasoning.

1. latitude, island, longitude, equator

Explain: ______________________

2. north, south, left, east

Explain: ______________________

3. ruler, globe, map, atlas

Explain: ______________________

4. compass rose, daisy, key, scale

Explain: ______________________

Name: ____________________ **Date:** ______________

Continental Crossword

A *continent* is a large body of land. There are seven continents on Earth.

Use the key words and the map to fill in the puzzle. Letters are shared when the words cross.

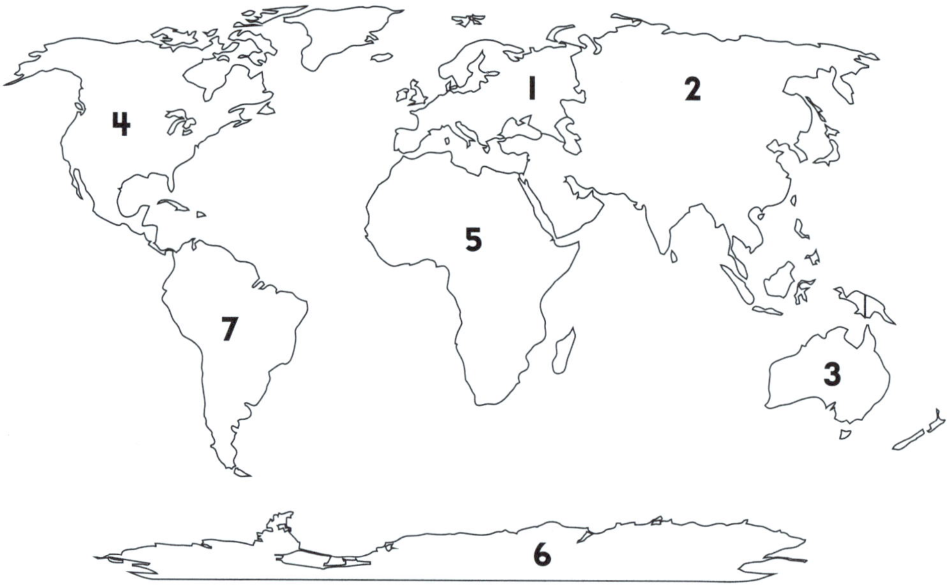

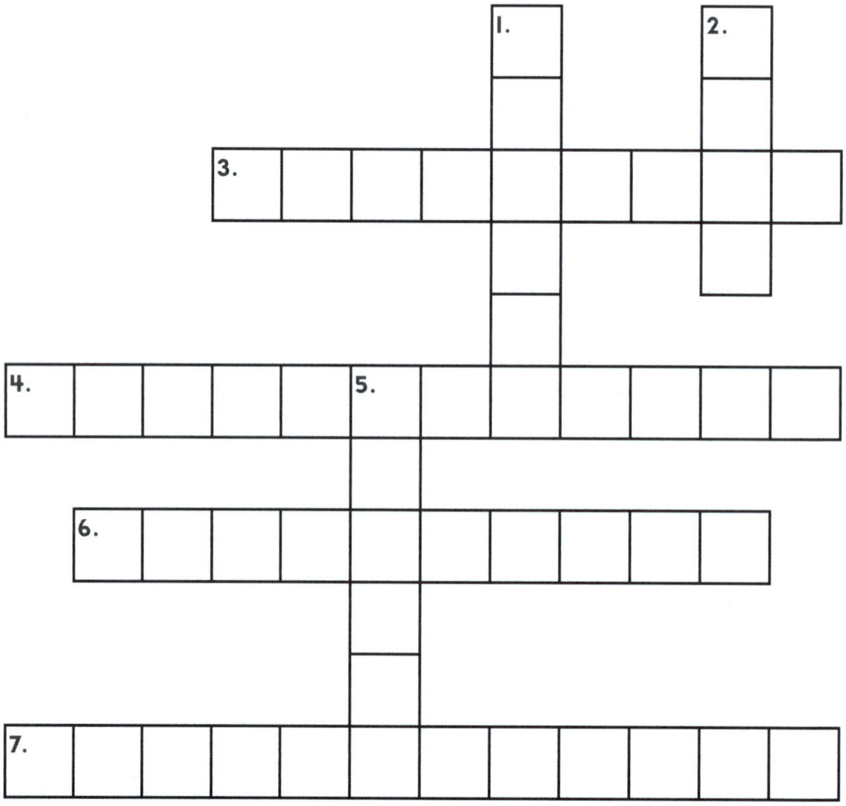

Name: ______________________ **Date:** ______________

Continent Code Cracker

What did one continent say to another?
Use the Code Breaker Key to find out.

CODE BREAKER KEY

A	B	C	D	E	F	G	H	I	J	K	L	M
N	**O**	**P**	**Q**	**R**	**S**	**T**	**U**	**V**	**W**	**X**	**Y**	**Z**

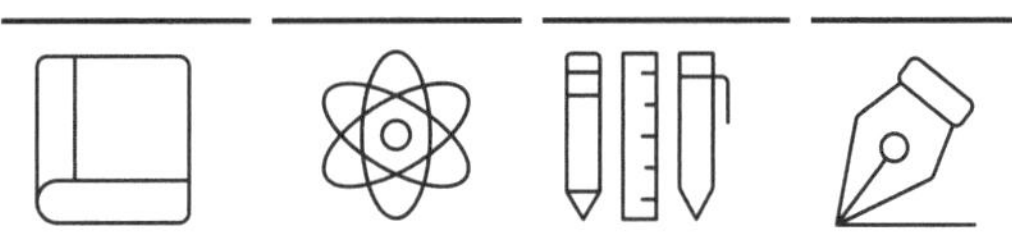

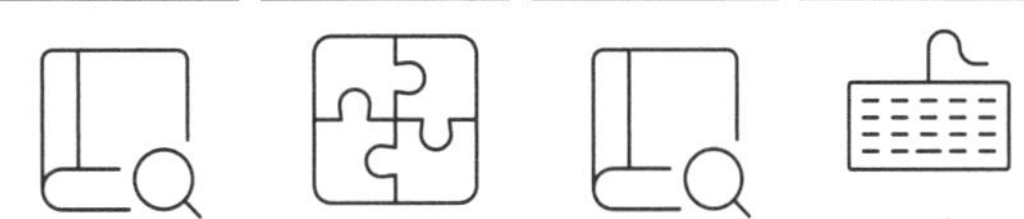

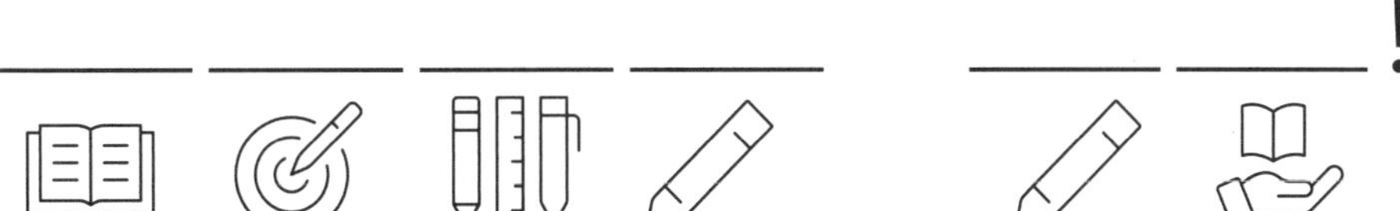

Name: ______________________________ **Date:** ______________

Name That Landform

Landforms are natural features of the Earth's surface, such as mountains, valleys, and glaciers.

KEY WORDS

canyon	**glacier**	**island**	**mountain**
ocean	**plateau**	**river**	**savanna**

Use the key words to answer the riddles below.

1. Not a mountain—no peaks that pop.
   I rise then level like a tabletop. ___ ___ ___ ___ ___ ___ ___

2. Deep and narrow, a rocky drop.
   Formed by a river that never stops. ___ ___ ___ ___ ___ ___

3. With twists and turns, I always go.
   Through canyons and plains, I rush and flow. ___ ___ ___ ___ ___

4. Sunny paradise by boat was found.
   Sandy land with water all around. ___ ___ ___ ___ ___ ___

5. I'm salty, deep, and stretch out far.
   I splash beneath each ray and star. ___ ___ ___ ___ ___

6. I may be slow, but I am strong.
   Frozen ice that glides along. ___ ___ ___ ___ ___ ___ ___

7. I'm the first to touch the sky,
   rocky tops where clouds drift by. ___ ___ ___ ___ ___ ___ ___ ___

8. Golden grass and ample sun,
   where wild animals roam for fun. ___ ___ ___ ___ ___ ___ ___

Name: ______________________ Date: ______________

Landform Logic

Read the definitions. Then unscramble the letters to spell each word.

KEY WORDS

canyon	**glacier**	**island**	**mountain**
ocean	**plateau**	**river**	**savanna**

1. nocnya ___ ___ (___) ___ ___ ___ — a deep, narrow valley with steep sides
2. vreir ___ ___ ___ (___) ___ — a long, flowing body of water
3. annsava ___ ___ (___) ___ ___ ___ ___ — flat, grassy land with very few trees
4. upealat ___ ___ (___) ___ ___ ___ ___ — flat land that is higher than the land around it
5. aiglrec ___ ___ ___ ___ ___ ___ (___) — a big, slow-moving sheet of ice
6. noeac ___ ___ (___) ___ ___ — a huge body of salty water
7. snalid ___ (___) ___ ___ ___ ___ — land with water all around it
8. nuniatmo ___ ___ ___ ___ (___) ___ ___ ___ — a large, high landform

Why is Mt. Everest always tired?
Write the circled letters in order to find out.

Because it can ___ ___ ___ ___ - ___ ___ ___ ___ !

Name: ______________________ Date: ______________

Three Parts of a Whole

The United States government is divided into three main groups. Each one has special powers and responsibilities.

KEY WORDS

branches	Congress	executive	judges
judicial	legislative	president	Senate

Use context clues to fill in the missing key word in each of the sentences.

1. The three parts of the government are also called (_) _ _ _ _ _ _ _, like parts of a tree.
2. The _ _ _ _ _ _ _ (_) _ is elected every four years and is the head of one of the branches.
3. That branch is the _ _ _ (_) _ _ _ _ _ branch.
4. The _ _ _ _ _ (_) _ _ _ _ _ branch makes laws.
5. Laws are made in the two houses of _ _ _ _ _ _ (_) _.
6. The _ _ _ (_) _ _ is one of those two houses.
7. The _ _ _ _ _ _ (_) _ branch makes sure laws follow the Constitution.
8. It includes _ _ _ _ (_) _ and the Supreme Court.

Unscramble the circled letters to complete this sentence.

This system provides checks and _ _ _ _ _ _ _ _ so no one branch has too much power.

Name: ______________________ **Date:** ______________

Branch Out

The United States government has three branches. They do different things, but they all work together to make our country run smoothly.

KEY WORDS

Congress	**court**	**houses**
judges	**justice**	**lawmakers**
president	**senator**	**veto**

Write each key word in the correct column. The main job of each branch is provided for you.

LEGISLATIVE	EXECUTIVE	JUDICIAL
makes laws	makes sure laws are obeyed	explains the laws

Name: ______________________________ **Date:** ________________

It's Election Day

Voting is an important right. Elections are how citizens of the United States choose leaders to speak for them and make laws.

KEY WORDS

ballot	campaign	candidate	citizens
election	political	polling	voter

Use the key words to complete the sentences below. You will use each word only once.

1. Signing up to vote is called ________________ registration.
2. United States ________________ can vote in local, state, and national elections.
3. Every four years, the United States has a presidential ________________ .
4. A ________________ is a person running for office.
5. During a ________________, candidates tell voters what they plan to do if they are elected.
6. Democrat and Republican are examples of ________________ parties.
7. Voters cast votes at a ________________ place.
8. They may vote electronically or use a ________________ box.

Name: ____________________ Date: ____________

Let's Vote!

Climb the word ladder to change *votes* into another word that relates to elections. Read each clue and follow the directions to create a new word.

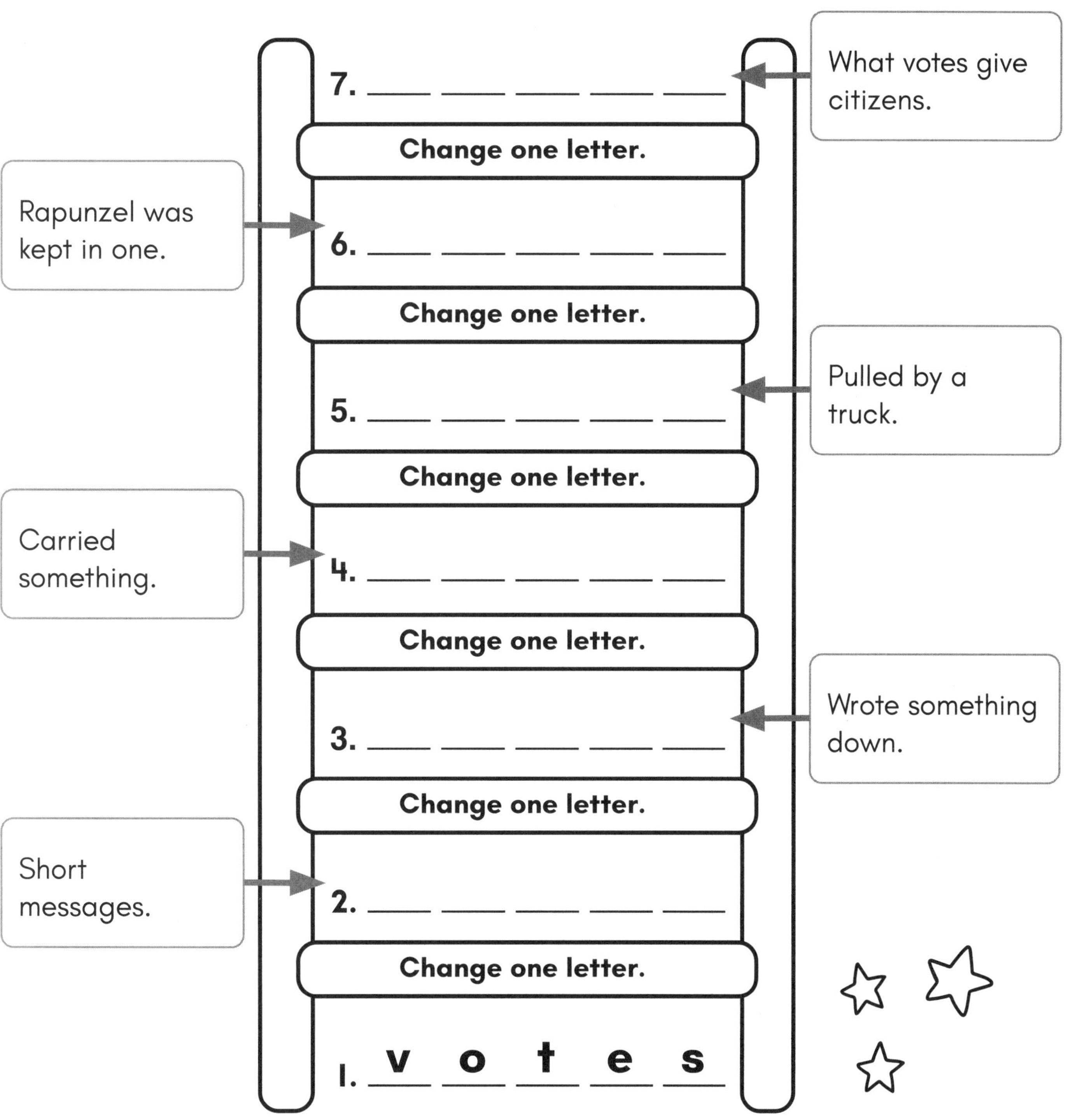

Name: ______________________ **Date:** ______________

Colonies in Reverse

The United States of America began with 13 colonies. Each colony helped shape the nation's early history.

Unscramble the letters to find the name of each of the 13 colonies. Then find that colony on the map and write its number in the correct box. The colonies are numbered from north to south.

- ☐ aiogGer ______________
- ☐ aiysnnavlneP ______________
- ☐ eralaDwe ______________
- ☐ cnoCitutcen ______________
- ☐ Nwe reyesJ ______________
- ☐ eNw rkYo ______________
- ☐ dynaMlar ______________
- ☐ weN ihspermHa ______________
- ☐ htroN aniloraC ______________
- ☐ suMesstatshca ______________
- ☐ uoSht loanraCi ______________
- ☐ edRoh dalsnI ______________
- ☐ iaVingri ______________

Name: ______________________ Date: ______________

Colonial Characteristics

Just like today's states, each of the original colonies had unique features, landforms, and communities.

KEY WORDS

Delaware	Georgia	Massachusetts
New York	North Carolina	South Carolina

Use the colony names to answer the riddles below.

1. Pilgrims landed on my shore, now I'm history to explore!

   ___ ___ ___ ___ ___ ___ ___ ___ ___ ___ ___ ___ ___

2. Great ships came to visit me, I grew into a colony by the sea.

   ___ ___ ___   ___ ___ ___ ___

3. I'm tiny, but I helped a lot. I'm near the bay—an awesome spot!

   ___ ___ ___ ___ ___ ___ ___ ___

4. The Lost Colony started here, near the ocean, wide and clear.

   ___ ___ ___ ___ ___   ___ ___ ___ ___ ___ ___ ___ ___

5. My rice and indigo grew so well, at Charleston port my ships did dwell.

   ___ ___ ___ ___ ___   ___ ___ ___ ___ ___ ___ ___ ___

6. I'm last but sunny near Florida's line, a place for peaches growing fine.

   ___ ___ ___ ___ ___ ___ ___

Write a sentence that tells something unique about your state.

____

Name: ______________________________ **Date:** ____________________

The Good Ol' Days

The way people lived long ago was very different from how we live today. For example, travel and communication were slower and more difficult then.

The things in the left column were all used long ago. Match each one with something we use today for the same purpose.

1. horse and buggy ●	● **A.** tractor
2. landline phone ●	● **B.** ballpoint pen
3. quill ●	● **C.** microwave
4. lantern ●	● **D.** laptop computer
5. ox and plow ●	● **E.** flashlight or LED light
6. sundial ●	● **F.** airplane or electric car
7. pony express ●	● **G.** interactive whiteboard
8. typewriter ●	● **H.** email or texts
9. woodstove ●	● **I.** smartphone
10. chalkboard ●	● **J.** smartwatch

Name: ______________________________ Date: ____________________

Search Through History

Find the key words in the puzzle. Circle the things that were used long ago. Draw rectangles around the things that we use today. Words can go → or ↓.

WORD BANK

drone	internet	lanterns	outhouse	quill
robot	smartphone	telegraph	texts	typewriter

w	t	y	p	e	w	r	i	t	e	r	g
t	e	x	t	s	m	g	w	j	y	q	d
l	a	n	t	e	r	n	s	h	c	u	r
r	o	u	t	h	o	u	s	e	h	i	o
o	o	l	o	r	o	q	a	t	j	l	n
b	t	e	l	e	g	r	a	p	h	l	e
o	s	m	a	r	t	p	h	o	n	e	b
t	i	n	t	e	r	n	e	t	d	v	z

Name: ______________________ Date: ______________

Greek Crisscross

Ancient Greece was the birthplace of many sports, arts, and ideas. Modern governments, buildings, and languages all have roots in ancient Greece.

Use the key words to fill in the puzzle. Letters are shared when the words cross.

KEY WORDS

- ancient
- Athens
- column
- democracy
- myth
- Olympics
- Parthenon
- philosopher

ACROSS

1. The capital city of Greece
4. A person who thinks and wonders about the big questions of life
6. A sporting event that began in Greece

DOWN

1. Very, very old
2. A pole or pillar that helps support a building
3. A government in which people choose their leaders by voting
4. An ancient temple on a hill in Athens
5. An old story about gods and heroes

Name: ______________________ Date: ______________

Socrates Says . . .

Socrates was a *philosopher*, or thinker, in ancient Greece. Use the Code Breaker Key to solve the puzzle and learn one of his famous sayings.

CODE BREAKER KEY

A	B	C	D	E	F	G	H	I	J	K	L	M
N	**O**	**P**	**Q**	**R**	**S**	**T**	**U**	**V**	**W**	**X**	**Y**	**Z**

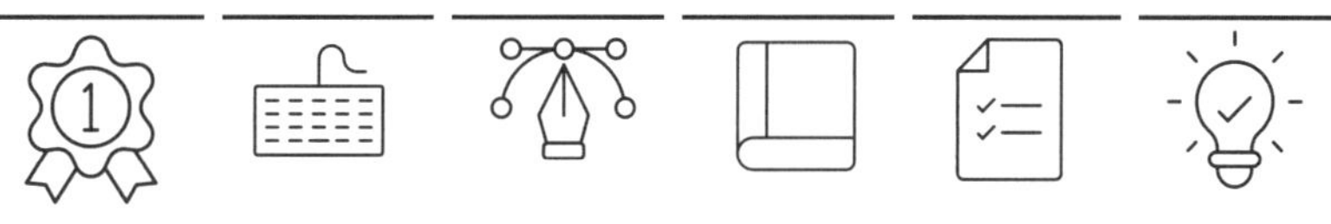

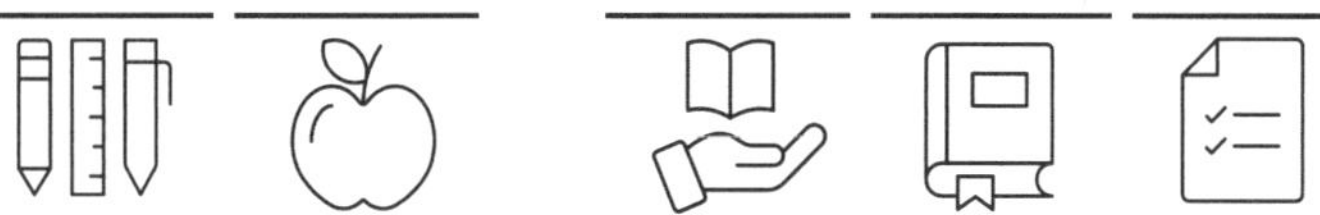

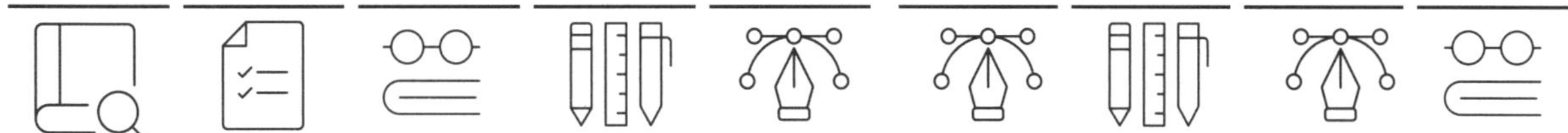

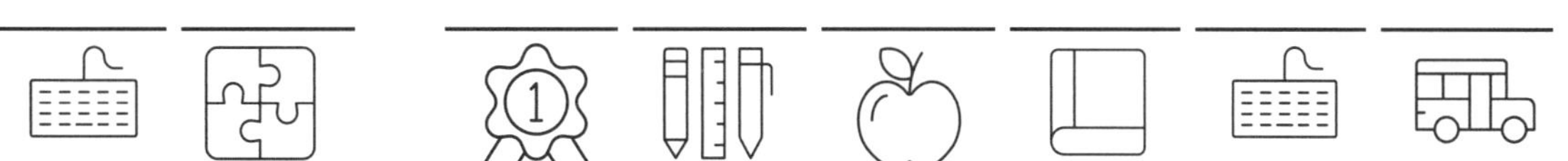

Name: ______________________ **Date:** ______________

Mummies and Mysteries

Ancient Egypt is the name for a large civilization of people who lived along the Nile River thousands of years ago.

KEY WORDS

gods	mummy	Nile	papyrus	pharaoh
pyramids	ruins	sphinx	temple	tomb

Use the key words to complete the sentences below. You will use each word only once.

1. A ___ ___ (___) ___ ___ ___ might honor a god or goddess.
2. People visit the old stone ___ (___) ___ ___ ___ to learn about the past.
3. The remains of King Tut were found deep inside his ___ ___ (___) ___ .
4. A ___ ___ (___) ___ ___ is a body that has been preserved.
5. Scribes wrote on a material called ___ ___ ___ (___) ___ ___ ___ .
6. Ancient Egyptians worshipped many ___ ___ ___ (___) and goddesses.
7. A ___ ___ (___) ___ ___ ___ has the head of a human, the body of a lion, and the wings of an eagle.
8. An ancient ruler of Egypt was called the ___ ___ ___ ___ ___ (___) ___ .
9. Ancient Egyptians built ___ ___ ___ ___ (___) ___ ___ ___ with triangle-shaped sides.
10. Along the banks of the River ___ ___ ___ (___) , crocodiles bask in the sun.

What did the pharaoh say when he saw the pyramid? Write the circled letters in order to find out.

___ ___ ___ ___ ___ ' ___ ___ ___ ___ ___ !

Name: ______________________ Date: ______________

A System of Writing

Ancient Egyptians wrote using picture symbols instead of words. Each picture stood for a word or a sound. The symbols included people, tools, and shapes. You can still see some of this writing today on ancient monuments and temples.

What are the symbols in this system of writing called?
Use the Code Breaker Key to find out.

CODE BREAKER KEY

A	B	C	D	E	F	G	H	I	J	K	L	M
N	O	P	Q	R	S	T	U	V	W	X	Y	Z

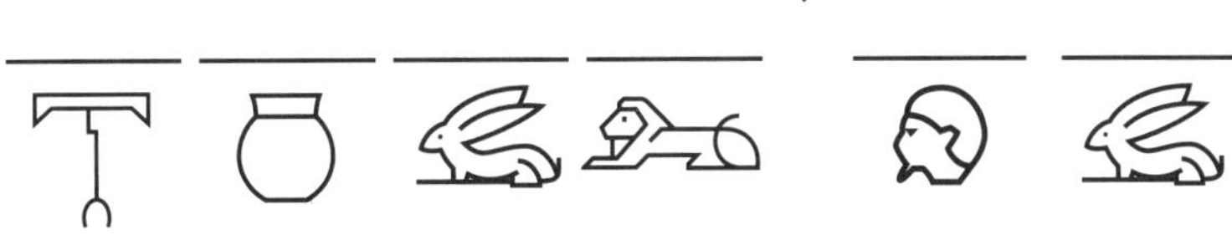

Answer Key

PAGE 8
1. about **2.** laugh **3.** would **4.** bring **5.** myself **6.** right **7.** very **8.** said; They help us *read* and *write* well.

PAGE 9

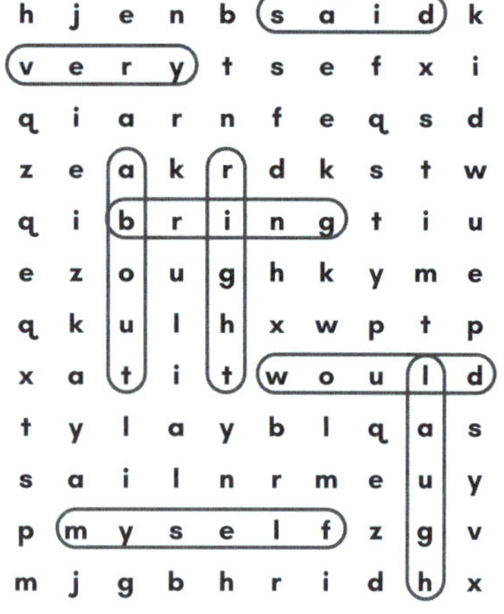

PAGE 10
1. around **2.** many **3.** few **4.** how **5.** where **6.** between **7.** below **8.** could

PAGE 11
Group colors and wording of explanations may vary.
RED GROUP: below, around, between; describe something's location
YELLOW GROUP: where, how, could; question words
BLUE GROUP: few, many, some; describe the amount of something

PAGE 12
1. D **2.** F **3.** B **4.** J **5.** C **6.** G **7.** A **8.** I **9.** H **10.** E

PAGE 13
underground, household, breakfast, ladybug, everywhere, folktale, doorbell, anthill, shoelace, afternoon; *Sample sentence:* The ladybug rang the doorbell.

PAGE 14
1. H **2.** I **3.** E **4.** B **5.** F **6.** C **7.** D **8.** G **9.** A; Sentences will vary. *Sample sentence:* I try to spell words right when I write.

PAGE 15
1. sent **2.** fairy **3.** board **4.** tow **5.** dough **6.** seen; Drawings will vary.

PAGE 16
Add *s*: birds, cats, giraffes, lizards
Add *es*: foxes, ostriches
Change *y* to *i* and add *es*: bunnies, guppies, ponies, puppies

PAGE 17
puppies, cats, hats, bunnies, buses, birds, iguanas, boxes, dishes

PAGE 18
PIRATES → it's → we're → I'm → they've → you're → he'll → she'll → can't → TREASURE

PAGE 19
1. I'm, C **2.** Leilani's, P **3.** You're, C **4.** he's, C **5.** elephants', P **6.** New York's, P **7.** she'd, C **8.** library's, P; Sentences will vary but must include the possessive noun *zebra's*.

PAGE 20
1. adjective **2.** adverb **3.** article **4.** conjunction **5.** noun **6.** preposition **7.** pronoun **8.** verb

PAGE 21
Check children's coloring: *big* and *silly* should be blue, *but* and *and* should be brown, *cat* and *house* should be green, *below* and *around* should be purple, *they* and *he* should be orange, *jump* and *walk* should be red

PAGE 22
1. owl **2.** ice **3.** turtle **4.** rocket **5.** giraffe **6.** cloud; Sentences will vary.

PAGE 23
Sentences will vary.

PAGE 24
1. D **2.** E **3.** H **4.** G **5.** B **6.** A **7.** I **8.** F **9.** C

PAGE 25
Group colors and wording of explanations may vary.
RED GROUP: lend a hand, cost an arm and a leg, cold feet; refer to body parts
YELLOW GROUP: busy as a bee, let the cat out of the bag, hold your horses; refer to animals
BLUE GROUP: on cloud nine, at the eleventh hour, two peas in a pod; include numbers

PAGE 26
ACROSS: 1. nonfiction **4.** graphic novel **6.** myth **7.** play **8.** fable
DOWN: 2. fiction **3.** folktale **5.** poetry

PAGE 27
1. FICTION **2.** NONFICTION **3.** PLAY **4.** POETRY

PAGE 28
1. fact **2.** primary **3.** authors **4.** secondary **5.** conclusion **6.** opinion **7.** research **8.** questions **9.** evidence; *Case closed!*

PAGE 29

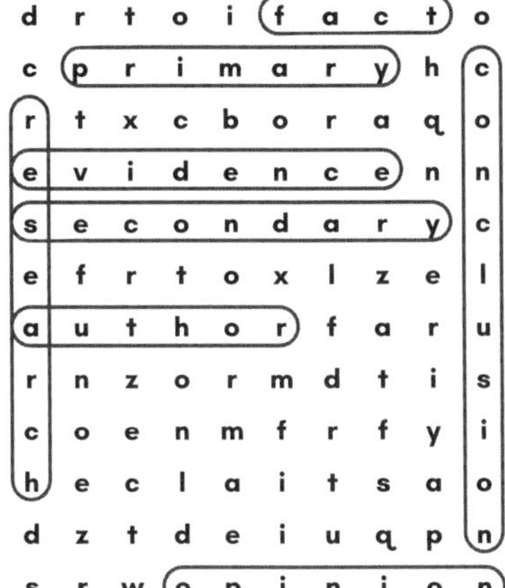

PAGE 30
persuade, inform, entertain; Drawings will vary.

PAGE 31
1. w (newspaper) **2.** r (story) **3.** i (recipe) **4.** t (articles) **5.** e (jokes) **6.** s (letters); An author *writes* to persuade, entertain, or inform.

PAGE 32
1. approach **2.** nervous **3.** invited **4.** tremble **5.** astonished **6.** exceptional **7.** pleasantly; *context*

PAGE 33
Sample answers: **1.** shy **2.** nice **3.** fun; Drawings will vary.

PAGE 34
1. trustworthy **2.** kind **3.** hardworking **4.** responsible **5.** fair **6.** honest **7.** cooperative **8.** thoughtful

PAGE 35
1. thoughtful **2.** fair **3.** honest **4.** responsible **5.** hardworking **6.** trustworthy **7.** kind **8.** cooperative

PAGE 36

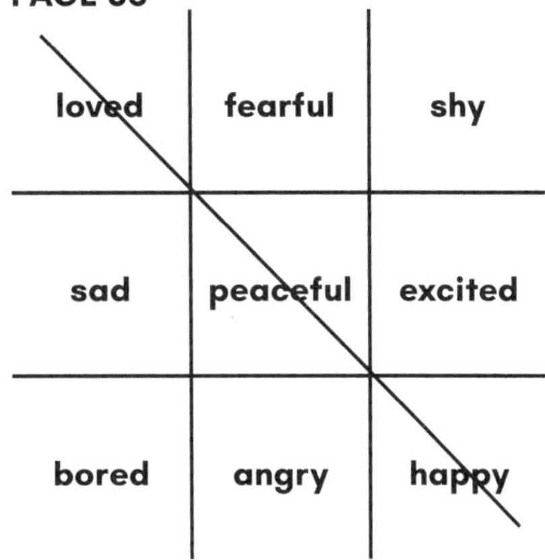

Drawings will vary.

PAGE 37
1. bored **2.** sad **3.** nervous **4.** grouchy **5.** excited **6.** peaceful **7.** happy **8.** love; Because they always *change*.

PAGE 38
1. E **2.** B **3.** H **4.** D **5.** F **6.** A **7.** C **8.** G

PAGE 39
1. calm **2.** surprised **3.** puzzled **4.** careful **5.** angry **6.** humiliated **7.** envious **8.** discouraged

PAGE 40
Sample answers: **1.** dark **2.** glad OR sad **3.** chilly OR hot **4.** quick OR slow **5.** huge OR small **6.** kind OR mean **7.** simple OR hard

PAGE 41
1. old **2.** polite **3.** push **4.** open **5.** slow **6.** in **7.** tall **8.** empty; *opposite*

PAGE 42
Real words may include: defrost, disagree, display, nonsense, preview, recycle, replay, review, unsafe

PAGE 43
The following words should be circled: nonstop, readjusted, previewed, rechecked, reread, unsure, discouraged; A *nonstop* hill!

PAGE 44
1. happy **2.** bravery **3.** fastest **4.** brave **5.** faster **6.** happiest **7.** bravely **8.** happiness **9.** fast

PAGE 45
Sample answers: action, cared, careful, careless, colorable, colored, colorful, colorless, collected, collectible, collection, dangerous, enjoyable, enjoyed, enjoy, helped, helpful, helpless, skilled, skillful, used, useful, useless, wondered, wonderful

PAGE 46
1. C **2.** B **3.** E **4.** F **5.** A **6.** D

PAGE 47
Sample answers: comport, conform, conscribe, deform, deport, describe, reform, report

PAGE 48
1. B **2.** A **3.** C **4.** F **5.** D **6.** G **7.** E

PAGE 49
Sample answers: audible, audience, audio, audiobook, audit, audition, auditor, auditorium, auditory; inspect, perspective, prospect, respect, retrospect, specification, specimen, spectacle, spectacular, spectator, spectrum, speculate; invisible, revise, supervise, television, visible, vision, visit, vista, visual

PAGE 50
1. gravity **2.** stem **3.** gas **4.** root **5.** solid **6.** planet **7.** liquid **8.** orbit

PAGE 51
Group colors and wording of explanations may vary.
RED GROUP: solid, liquid, gas; states of matter
YELLOW GROUP: leaf, stem, root; parts of a plant
BLUE GROUP: gravity, planet, orbit; relate to space

PAGE 52
Answers will vary but should include at least two of the key words.

PAGE 53

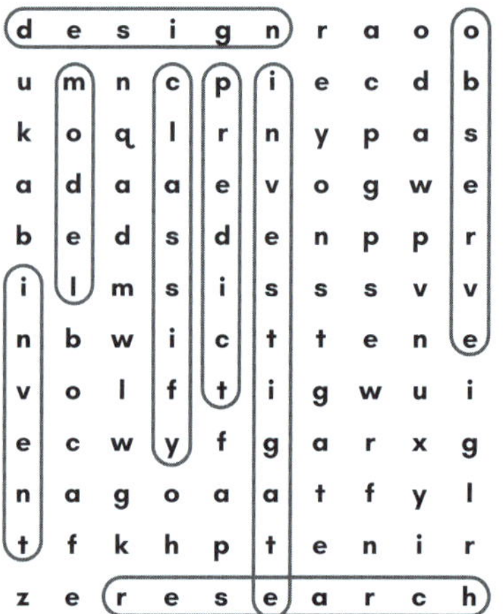

PAGE 54
1. botanist, plants **2.** ecologist, the planet **3.** geologist, rocks
4. meteorologist, weather
5. paleontologist, fossils **6.** zoologist, animals

PAGE 55
Answers will vary. *Sample sentence:* I chose zoologist because I love animals.

PAGE 56
1. freshwater **2.** grassland
3. seashore **4.** wetland **5.** riverbank
6. mountaintop **7.** woodland; We call them compound words.

PAGE 57
1. t (wetland) **2.** i (rivers)
3. m (mountain) **4.** e (freshwater)
5. g (grassland) **6.** o (forest);
Time to go!

PAGE 58
ACROSS: 2. seed **4.** reproduce
6. adult **7.** metamorphosis
DOWN: 1. larva **2.** sprout **3.** pupa
5. offspring

PAGE 59
Group colors and wording of explanations may vary.
RED GROUP: larva, caterpillar, butterfly; butterfly life cycle stages
YELLOW GROUP: egg, chick, hen; chicken life cycle stages
BLUE GROUP: tadpole, froglet, frog; frog life cycle stages

PAGE 60
1. survive **2.** camouflage **3.** habitat
4. behavior **5.** adapt **6.** mimicry
7. traits **8.** inherit; Because they don't have *suitcases.*

PAGE 61

m	e	j	a	s	t	r	a	i	t
w	u	j	g	f	x	d	c	d	g
r	c	l	l	m	z	i	a	i	r
b	e	q	p	v	e	k	m	n	q
e	o	p	m	i	s	o	o	h	l
h	v	w	i	h	u	b	u	e	x
a	n	t	m	a	r	a	f	r	t
v	r	i	i	b	v	u	l	i	g
i	s	u	c	i	l	g	a	t	r
o	u	i	r	t	v	l	g	d	u
r	m	j	y	a	e	l	e	e	e
a	d	a	p	t	g	a	z	t	j

PAGE 62
1. position **2.** friction **3.** gravity
4. direction **5.** accelerate **6.** motion
7. speed **8.** force

PAGE 63
1. *run* should be circled; it is not a force of motion **2.** *grow* should be circled; the other words are all types of movement **3.** *planet* should be circled; the others are all simple machines that move things **4.** *color* should be circled; it is not related to motion

PAGE 64
1. north **2.** repel **3.** south **4.** attract
5. pole **6.** magnet **7.** compass
8. field

PAGE 65

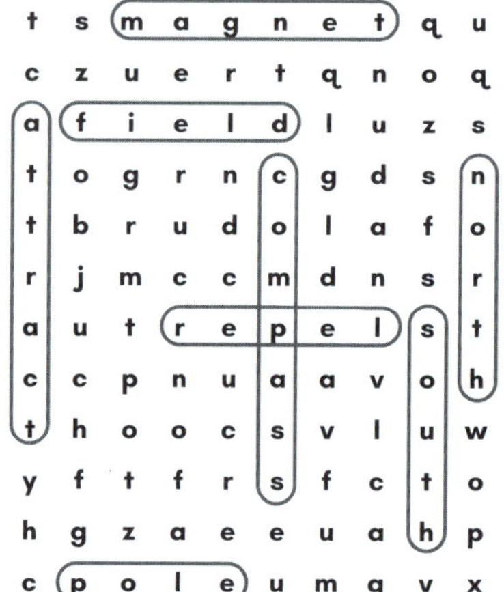

PAGE 66
ACROSS: 5. precipitation **6.** melt
7. boil **8.** evaporation
DOWN: 1. vapor **2.** water cycle
3. condensation **4.** freeze

PAGE 67
GOODBYE! YOU WILL BE MIST!

PAGE 68
1. fossil **2.** extinct **3.** bones **4.** amber
5. skeleton **6.** sediment

PAGE 69
1. amber **2.** fossil **3.** sediment
4. skeleton **5.** extinct **6.** bones

PAGE 70
Sample answers: ants, art, ate, date, deny, dine, dirt, dreamiest, dry, earn, entry, mastery, mat, mate, meat, men, mine, mint, name, near, nest, net, rat, rate, read, red, remains, rest, sad, sand, sat, seat, sediment, send, set, smartened, stain, star, stem, stir, tame, tan, tar, tea, tear, ten, tie, time, tin, tire, train, trained, tray, tree, try, yard, year

PAGE 71
1. shale **2.** scale **3.** scare **4.** score **5.** shore **6.** shone **7.** stone

PAGE 72
ACROSS: 1. shelter **2.** flood **5.** emergency **6.** hail **7.** tornado
DOWN: 1. snow **2.** forecast **3.** drought **4.** weather

PAGE 73
BE A RAINBOW IN SOMEONE ELSE'S CLOUD.

PAGE 74
1. vapor **2.** droplets **3.** crystals **4.** clouds **5.** rain **6.** snowflakes **7.** sleet **8.** hail

PAGE 75
1. rain **2.** gain **3.** main **4.** mail **5.** nail **6.** tail **7.** hail

PAGE 76
ACROSS: 4. garbage **5.** reduce **7.** pollution
DOWN: 1. environment **2.** landfill **3.** reuse **5.** recycle **6.** cleanup

PAGE 77
REDUCE, REUSE, AND RECYCLE.

PAGE 78
1. C **2.** F **3.** B **4.** E **5.** A **6.** D

PAGE 79
Sample answers: deduce, demand, deport, detract, export, extract, induce, induct, produce, protract

PAGE 80
1. *firefighter* should be circled; the others are workers at a school **2.** *boat* should be circled; the others are groups of people **3.** *fly* should be circled; the other words are things a community does together **4.** *river* should be circled; the other words are locations of communities

PAGE 81
Answers will vary.

PAGE 82
PIRATES → Voting in elections → Speaking freely → Being treated fairly → Having access to food → Getting help in emergencies → Drinking clean water → Being safe → Practicing your religion → TREASURE

PAGE 83
1. rule **2.** equal **3.** leader **4.** respect **5.** task **6.** kindness **7.** share **8.** effort **9.** tools **10.** safety

PAGE 84
NEEDS: food, safety, shelter, water
WANTS: bicycle, camera, phone, toys, truck

PAGE 85
1. (c)(camera) **2.** e (water) **3.** (h)(phone) **4.** l (shelter) **5.** (o)(toys) **6.** d (food) **7.** (r)(truck) **8.** (e)(bicycle); *chore*

PAGE 86
1. goods **2.** consumer **3.** producer **4.** supply **5.** economy **6.** earn **7.** money **8.** service

PAGE 87
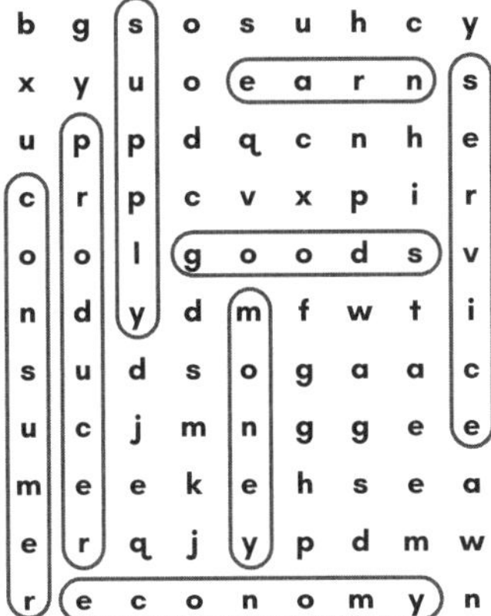

PAGE 88
1. truck **2.** train **3.** motorcycle **4.** airplane **5.** ferry **6.** helicopter **7.** ship **8.** vehicle **9.** bus; *Time flies!*

PAGE 89
1. bike **2.** bite **3.** mite **4.** mitt **5.** mist **6.** most **7.** cost **8.** cast **9.** cart

PAGE 90
1. globe **2.** latitude **3.** rose **4.** poles **5.** scale **6.** equator **7.** borders **8.** cardinal **9.** key **10.** miles

PAGE 91
1. *island* should be circled; the other words are reference lines on a globe **2.** *left* should be circled; the other words are cardinal directions on a map **3.** *ruler* should be circled; the other words are tools that show geographical features **4.** *daisy* should be circled; the other words refer to map features

PAGE 92
ACROSS: 3. Australia **4.** North America **6.** Antarctica **7.** South America
DOWN: 1. Europe **2.** Asia **5.** Africa

PAGE 93
STOP DRIFTING AWAY FROM ME!

PAGE 94
1. plateau **2.** canyon **3.** river
4. island **5.** ocean **6.** glacier
7. mountain **8.** savanna

PAGE 95
1. canyon **2.** river **3.** savanna
4. plateau **5.** glacier **6.** ocean
7. island **8.** mountain; Because it can *neva-rest!*

PAGE 96
1. branches **2.** president **3.** executive
4. legislative **5.** Congress **6.** Senate
7. judicial **8.** judges; This system provides checks and *balances* so no one branch has too much power.

PAGE 97
LEGISLATIVE: Congress, houses, lawmakers, senator
EXECUTIVE: president, veto
JUDICIAL: court, judges, justice

PAGE 98
1. voter **2.** citizens **3.** election
4. candidate **5.** campaign
6. political **7.** polling **8.** ballot

PAGE 99
1. votes **2.** notes **3.** noted **4.** toted
5. towed **6.** tower **7.** power

PAGE 100
13. Georgia **7.** Pennsylvania
8. Delaware **4.** Connecticut
6. New Jersey **5.** New York
9. Maryland **2.** New Hampshire
11. North Carolina **1.** Massachusetts
12. South Carolina **3.** Rhode Island
10. Virginia

PAGE 101
1. Massachusetts **2.** New York
3. Delaware **4.** North Carolina
5. South Carolina **6.** Georgia;
Sentences will vary.

PAGE 102
1. F **2.** I **3.** B **4.** E **5.** A **6.** J **7.** H
8. D **9.** C **10.** G

PAGE 103
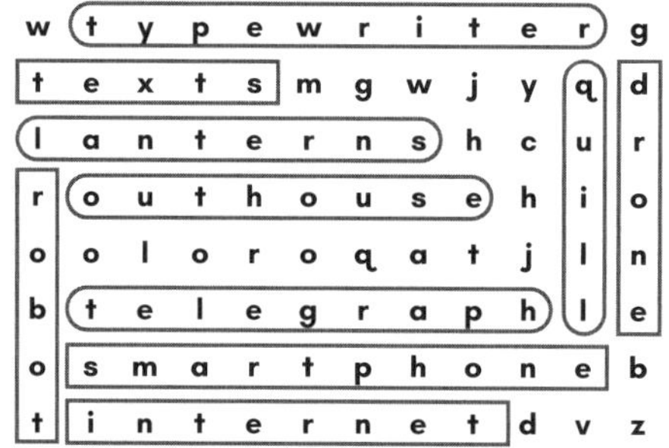

w	t	y	p	e	w	r	i	t	e	r	g
t	e	x	t	s	m	g	w	j	y	q	d
l	a	n	t	e	r	n	s	h	c	u	r
r	o	u	t	h	o	u	s	e	h	i	o
o	o	l	o	r	o	q	a	t	j	l	n
b	t	e	l	e	g	r	a	p	h	l	e
o	s	m	a	r	t	p	h	o	n	e	b
t	i	n	t	e	r	n	e	t	d	v	z

PAGE 104
ACROSS: 1. Athens **4.** philosopher
6. Olympics
DOWN: 1. ancient **2.** column
3. democracy **4.** Parthenon **5.** myth

PAGE 105
WONDER IS THE BEGINNING OF WISDOM.

PAGE 106
1. temple **2.** ruins **3.** tomb **4.** mummy
5. papyrus **6.** gods **7.** sphinx
8. pharaoh **9.** pyramids **10.** Nile;
Mummy's home!

PAGE 107
THEY'RE CALLED HIEROGLYPHS.